THE NEWLY

BOOK OF P

# THE NEWLY DIVORCED BOOK OF PROTOCOL

*How to Be Civil When You Hate Their Guts*

by
Gloria Lintermans

Barricade Books Inc.
New York

Published by Barricade Books Inc.
150 Fifth Avenue
New York, NY 10011

Printed in the United States of America.

Library of Congress Cataloging-in-Publication Data

Lintermans, Gloria.
    The newly divorced book of protocol / Gloria Lintermans.
        p.   cm.
    ISBN 1-56980-037-5 (cloth) : $17.95
    1. Divorce. 2. Divorced people—Psychology. I. Title.
  HQ814.L73   1995
306.89—dc20                                                     94-44570
    Second Printing                              ￼                    CIP

There are so many people to whom my thanks is richly deserved. Contributors all, I applaud you.

To Carole Stuart, for her understanding of, and belief in, this project; to Sandra Lee Stuart, my editor at Barricade Books, for her help and support in shaping the vision of this book and bringing it to fruition;

To the many men and women who so generously shared their stories of hurt and triumph, you have my gratitude and admiration. Without your willingness to let us see your pain and to share in your courage, this book would never have been possible;

To the many mental-health-care professionals willing to *really* listen to my questions and offer their invaluable insight so that we all might benefit;

To Ellie, who gave me the courage to dive in, kept me from drowning, and heralded my triumphs all along the way—for once, words fail me. Your love and knowledge were indispensable;

To Gail, Lynn, and Leslie—loving friends each, who in their own dear way provided the support and encouragement I grew to understand were so much a part of this project;

To Richard and Evan, my sons, for whom this book is written with such love;

And, to Rick, my life partner, who helped to keep my body and soul together throughout a process which included distraction, joy, and (metaphorically speaking) just a little nail biting.

# TABLE OF CONTENTS

# Introduction

Maybe you know someone who's had an amazingly civil divorce. No ugly scenes, vile language, or getting the other person where it hurts. Do these people exist?

Now that divorce is happening to you, the important thing, you think, is to just get through it. Style isn't important when you're feeling this raw. Wrong! You're not alone in this mess. There are children, in-laws, parents, sisters, brothers, aunts, and uncles to consider. Even your old friends.

Divorce is a family affair and more often than not, especially when children are involved, a horror. Don't get me wrong, children aren't the problem. There's just so much more to fight about with children in the picture, and for so much longer. But parents you were, and parents you'll be, irrevocably and forever . . . tied to one another, in this case, for better or worse.

This is an etiquette book, of sorts. It seems once divorce begins, good manners often are lost. Yet, good manners keep us secure, not only as a society but individually. Rules and regulations take you from separation to final decree without POWs or casualties, especially the children.

Here, those who have gone before you look back with the objective eye only time can bring, realizing they could have done it better and that no, they didn't die from the pain.

These real-life people and their stories will help you to know that even intelligent people do stupid things when they're afraid and hurting. Perhaps an occasional laugh of recognition will help, too, as these people share their stories and newfound wisdom.

In addition, family counselors may provide a gentle nudge or worthwhile advice on how to navigate emotional currents.

Divorce begins with the predecision phase, a time of emotional detachment from your spouse. Next comes the decision phase, when physical separation begins. That's followed by the mourning phase, when feelings of emotional pain, anger, guilt, and self-reproach surface and become part of a long period of adjustment. And finally, the time comes to find a new balance, a time of growth as the past falls into perspective.

Although every stage is wrenching, the struggle need not involve everyone around you. Divorce is hard enough, so why compound it with inexcusably bad behavior? You both need all the love and support you can get from friends and family.

Where do you start? It may help to know you are not alone. More than 40 percent of all marriages in the United States now end in divorce. More than half of all divorces involve children. When children are concerned, it is important to remember that divorce ends your role of spouse, not that of parent.

It is comforting that most children of divorced parents eventually adjust, but sad to note that others do not and suffer long-term depression. For some families, leftover anger gets in the way of recovery, while for others divorce becomes a vehicle for growth. For most, the choice is yours.

Children and their parents do not necessarily adjust at the same rate. Some children do so before their parents, sometimes the reverse. A child may continue to suffer, even though his parents have come to terms with the divorce and are building new lives. Then, too, children within a family may respond differently, one child gaining maturity and independence, another regressing.

The divorce process is hurtful for everyone. Rarely do both spouses want the divorce or, if so, seldom are they ready for it at the same time. The "left" spouse may feel an acute loss of self-esteem, rage, anxiety, shock, and very often bitterness. The spouse wanting the divorce may also go through a time of emotional stress, feeling lonely, guilty, or disappointed if the divorce doesn't solve problems or meet expectations for happiness.

Here are the nuts and bolts of surviving day-to-day situations. A guide for navigating tricky situations without everyone you know wanting to jump ship.

"In Our Family We Don't Divorce Our Men—We Bury Them."

*Ruth Gordon, actress*

# PART ONE

## DETACHMENT

"He's The Kind Of Man A Woman Would Have To Marry
To Get Rid Of."

*Mae West*

# CHAPTER ONE

## *The Secret*

*You know it. Your spouse probably knows it. You're just not ready to know it together.*

Divorce is an unfortunate fact in many lives. Perhaps in your life. And, maybe divorce is not even the best solution to a troubled marriage, except in cases of abuse. But whether you do the leaving, or are the one left, or the decision is by mutual consent—divorce ranks with death of a loved one in terms of grief and suffering.

It's even been said that death may be easier to bear. Death is final, offering emotional closure after a healthy period of grieving. A period in which friends and family not only support but encourage your grief. The love you feel for your lost spouse is honored, even held in admiration. But divorce is angry, ugly, divisive, even unclean. You can expect, at best, a limited time of support and handholding from friends and family before you are expected to get over your fury and get on with your life.

"I've been married for almost fourteen years and have often contemplated divorce," says Jennifer. "The reason I've hesitated is because I hate the idea of my fate being in the hands of a judge and lawyers. My husband's income is much more substantial than mine. With his financial resources, I'm afraid that he can keep the divorce process going for years, until I run out of money to fight him further."

Many people falsely think that divorce begins when one of you leaves. But emotionally, divorce begins long before the moving van pulls up. Just getting ready to say you're leaving can take days or years. That's one reason divorce is so emotionally devastating. During this time of distancing yourself, many different feelings may surface, including anger, resentment, bitterness, and jealousy—in varying degrees depending on what day it is.

"I knew my marriage was terminal for a long, long time. But 'terminal' meant it could linger," says Sharon. "Now I look back and recall indicators: like when the garage door opened, my nervous system reactions—my stomach twisted, and I got keyed up. I didn't like him . . . I tried to, but it was only after I threw in the towel that I gave myself permission not to like him. In hindsight, I should have left years and years ago, but how do you know? I rationalized a lot of things to avoid the pain, and hurt, and the awareness. I guess I knew, but resisted the feeling.

"I found that once I actually made the decision, I felt a lot less struggle in my life. Before I remember second guessing every decision or judgment I made. My ex did me a favor. He pushed and abused our relationship with such brutality that I snapped."

Typically, you know you're leaving. It's just a matter of when. You're even sure your spouse knows it on some unspoken level.

"At the time of my divorce, I had two young children," says Rebecca. "Some would say that was reason enough to hold any marriage together that wasn't abusive. But I was miserable and desperately wanted out. I felt like a jerk, wanting to tear my family apart."

A career woman, Rebecca continues, "I was sure that if I could just hang in there long enough, he'd get the idea and petition the breakup. Then, it could be his fault! Unfortunately, he never did get it, or if he did, was willing to wait out the storm. I kept stuffing my emotions further and further down. It was hell not having the nerve to tell him. I woke daily with the words on the tip of my tongue and went to sleep each night thinking—tomorrow I'll tell him. And, during all this time, about a year, I convinced myself that I was staying with him to avoid upsetting the children.

"So what did I do? I stopped breathing. Asthma. The medication the doctor doled out kept me borderline unconscious. I lost weight, the children were miserable. Did he blindly believe all was well? I think not. But as long as I didn't talk about it, he was able to ignore what was going on. I couldn't believe he didn't know. The secret was literally making me sick."

Katherine says, "My parents had an unhappy marriage so I entered mine without giving much thought to my own happiness. Thinking back, I don't believe I even liked my husband.

"I functioned without much emotion through the first six years of my eight-year marriage, except that my two children did bring me happiness. The boredom and emptiness of my marriage prompted me to return to college. I quickly developed an infatuation for my psychology teacher and had an affair with him. While I felt guilty about this relationship, it taught me I had feelings I never knew existed and made it impossible for me to continue to live my life without them.

"It took me another year to separate from my husband. I didn't speak much about my unhappiness with him, knowing he wouldn't have been able to understand me anyway. I also didn't tell him about the affair because I knew he wouldn't be able to tolerate my infidelity. Although I was the one to leave our marriage, I feel he was partly responsible for the breakup because he wouldn't consider my needs."

Like Rebecca, Wendy says, "It took me about six months to work up the courage to finally tell my husband I was leaving. I don't know why I was so scared to tell him. It wasn't that I feared physical abuse of any kind. I just couldn't do it. Finally I rented an apartment for myself and my little girl. Did I tell him then? Nope! When? The day I packed."

WHAT ABOUT THE CHILDREN? Don't fool yourself. The children know something's up—and that it's not good. While to your neighbors it may look as if everything is normal, a great deal of emotional distancing is going on, which is the prelude to action. Unless you're an emotional robot, or living with blinders, one very disturbing thing is happening: tension so thick you can almost touch it.

Rusty Horn, M.S., a Manhattan psychotherapist and psychoanalyst, offers these suggestions for helping your children through this time.

"Don't try to hide the truth. Children are very sensitive. Even if they don't know things consciously, they sense something is wrong.

"Talk with them about relationships. Explain that just because you love somebody, that doesn't necessarily mean a marriage will work out. Relationships require problem-solving efforts, hard work, as well as a basic compatibility. You can't always know in the beginning if two people can be happy and compatible together. Tell your children you love them and that you will not stop loving them. Keep in mind that children feel most secure when their parents are happy together. Divorce threatens that.

"Reassure them that after you separate, they will still have two parents. Assure them that husband and wife roles are different from the roles of mother and father. They will still have a mother and father, even if husband and wife are no longer a team.

"As a couple, and for your children, explore every avenue which might help you work out the relationship. Determine if individual problems are standing in the way or whether they are truly problems of compatibility. Is the problem with you or the relationship? Try to be certain. You're not just breaking up a marriage but a family, and that can be very difficult for everyone," says Horn. "If you are unsure, speaking with a professional trained to look beneath the surface for motivations could be helpful." Or, you may find the advice of a neutral third party, such as your clergyman, of benefit.

"Reassure your children, it's not their fault," continues Horn. "Children are mostly egocentric, they think they are the center of the universe, and therefore the cause of everything. Tell them it's a big enough job just for them to grow up and learn to be themselves. They don't have to take care of their parents, too."

They have no choice in what's happening, yet are probably the most affected by what's going on. The trick is to remember, you are still a parent despite the fact that you're feeling confused and distraught. Workable rules between you and your partner will help the children feel cared for and secure. If you feel lost, just imagine how they must feel. Make a deal with your spouse to honor rules that keep your children's lives as stable as possible during this very unstable time.

When divorce involves children, it is doubly difficult. But, even without them, the decision is no less heart wrenching. "While I had no children to consider," says Steve, "I was still very much afraid of leaving. Despite the fact that it had been a painful and very unfulfilling relationship, leaving was difficult for me.

"I had never really been on my own, and the divorce stigma was a real thing to me. I finally resolved that I was more miserable staying than I was afraid of leaving. While it was scary to go out on my own, there was also the chance of starting my life over. That prospect, a new start, a new life, and maybe finding someone with whom I could be happy, helped me more than anything.

"I knew that if I stayed, I would be with someone who refused to recognize the trouble in our marriage and with whom I would never have the happy and loving relationship I saw in many of my friends. I finally realized I didn't have to go on like that forever; my life could change, and I'am glad I made that step."

## Suggestions

*Do* acknowledge that the decision to leave is, and should be, difficult.

*Do* be aware of your children and their needs during this time.

*Don't* assume that by pretending nothing's going on that you, or your children, can continue with life as usual without snowballing tension.

*Don't* assume your children don't know something awful is going on just because you're not talking about it.

# CHAPTER TWO

## *Straddling the Doorstep*
*Home isn't an "in-n-out" burger place.*
*-and-*

## *Paralyzing Fear*
*What if there isn't someone—or something—better*
*out there!*

The words "breaking up," imply a clean—one day you're to-gether, the next you're not—situation. In truth, breaking up is rarely that. It's neither clean nor quick. It's as if a couple is held together by saltwater taffy. As you begin to pull apart, the taffy stretches until a bit at a time it breaks, or snaps. Piece by piece, you begin to tear. It can be as emotionally horrendous as it would be physically to lose parts of your body, inch by inch. Especially so when your spouse leaves more than once.

As Lydia, a woman in her midthirties, found out all too well. "We were married in 1971 and divorced in 1988. During that time I'm pretty sure my husband fooled around, certainly for the last five years of our marriage. Even though he tried to hide it, his behavior was suspicious. The first time I realized he might have a girlfriend was when I started finding blonde hair on his jacket. Also, the phone would ring at six a.m. (sometimes during the week—other times during the weekend), he'd answer, jump out of bed, get dressed, and, like a flash, run out the door. Even though he normally left for work early in the morning, I started checking the mileage on his car. A pattern began to emerge. He was driving only a mile and a half away, a much shorter distance than his drive to the office. I knew that wherever he was going, it wasn't far."

Then his office Christmas list arrived, with the names and addresses of the staff, and coincidentally there was a listing for a woman who lived, you guessed it, about a mile and a half away! Putting two and two together wasn't hard for Lydia.

"The following Sunday, after a 6 a.m. call, I got in my car and drove to her apartment. Not realizing he'd parked two blocks away, I didn't see his car. So I went to a gas station and called. She answered the phone but hung up on me. I don't know what drove me to do it, but I went back to her apartment and knocked on the door. She answered the door in her bathrobe." Recalling it now with a chuckle, Lydia explained how she "just pushed her aside, marched right in, and there he was, hiding—no, cowering—in a corner of the kitchen."

Later that day Lydia and her husband had a long talk, and he explained that he and his girlfriend were in the process of breaking up. After a week or two, he told Lydia that it was over. Remember, all this time he was still living at home.

"Then, to my complete surprise, he moved out. I came home from work one day, and he was gone. He left a note explaining that *he* 'couldn't take it anymore.' I felt horrible—abandoned and betrayed. In fact, he'd moved just two blocks away, although he was no longer with that woman. We continued to communicate and within a few months, he moved back in. I thought we'd try again.

"Surprise—he moved out again! This time taking everything, every stick of furniture! He kissed me good-bye in the morning, saying 'you look beautiful.' He said that he wasn't going to go to work, he was going fishing with the guys, to a tournament. I thought, that's nice and told him I'd have dinner ready. He said that wouldn't be necessary. When I got home that night, he and practically everything else in the house was gone. Even though I had known that he was still somewhat distant, and that things weren't right, I was shocked. I had thought we were starting to communicate again and that things were slowly getting better. Obviously not.

"About six months later, a friend was at the market, and there he was with a baby in his cart, his baby. A baby conceived while he was still living with me."

The decision to stay together or part might feel like one you make alone, but divorce is a process which must be shared. To simply disappear adds layers of hurt and betrayal to a family already in chaos. It takes all the courage and maturity we possess to work together during this time. The alternative will send ripples of destruction through every area of your life.

"I was married for a number of years. Sadly," says Sharon, a college professor, "his pattern of taking off began after the first eighteen months. After he left a few times, we lived apart for a full year. During that year of separation, we did manage to see each other pretty often. I can remember at least four times rebuilding the relationship to a point where he would move back in. We even filed for dissolution until he decided that he wanted our marriage more than a divorce."

Unfortunately, no matter how much Sharon and her husband tried to talk it through, she couldn't erase the feelings of shock and panic she had felt coming home from work to find all of his belongings missing. Each time, she had been left with an overwhelming and enormous emptiness. "What did I do wrong? Why did he do that? Why is he punishing me? Am I going crazy or have I been crazy all along? Can I live through this, and what is this I'm living through?"

Hoping to find reasons, and solutions, Sharon went back into their history. She rationalized, came up with many awful experiences they had shared that might have chased him away. The miscarriage of a child, months of fertility specialists, tests, seminars, waiting, and disappointments. Then, an adoption attorney and a birthmother who took advantage of them and ran, leaving them emotionally and monetarily depleted.

"But, I'd shared those heartbreaks and disappointments and hadn't run away. The first few hours and days after his abandonments are vivid. I remember such physical pain, I could almost hear my heart pound. I couldn't sleep. I would go from hurt, to rage, to loneliness, to missing him—and back again, so often and so fast I was sure I was going crazy.

"I tried to take control of my life, I thought. I found out where he'd arranged to have his mail sent and staked out the area for any sign of him.

"The last time, it was quite a while before we saw each other, even though he telephoned. He kept his distance and unavailability—all frightening to me. This warm, loving man I had married had become a cold, hard statue."

These situations are difficult even without children to care for. Is it an overgenerous or naive heart which allows a spouse to come back over and over again? Or, a fear of being alone? Can emotional intimacy be maintained? Even if you do open your door again and again, without trust, intimacy dies.

Equally important, during all the turmoil, who's caring for the children? Family counselor, Jennifer Andrews, Ph.D., of Los Angeles, advises, "Talk to your children about what's going on. No matter where they're living, provide them with continuing access—including the ability to contact you by phone—if possible, even at work. Children take their emotional clues from the adults around them, so be aware that they'll be acutely conscious of yours."

Children from two-parent marriages may soon be in the minority. About a million children a year in the United States experience a broken home and the attendant problems of having only one live-in parent. When a parent leaves more than once, it is even more important to be open, to talk about what's happening, and to ask, as well as observe, how your children are doing.

What causes some people to leave, leave, and then, leave again before it sticks? A paralyzing fear that goes something like this. *What if there really isn't a someone—or something—better for me out there?* This terror contributes to the "in-and-out" dance you, or your partner, may have orchestrated.

*What if there's no one else out there, and you'll be alone for the rest of your life?* This fear can also trigger other harmful behaviors, and women and men alike start doing some pretty stupid things. For instance? Flirting shamelessly with every member of the opposite sex (including your best friend's husband, your boss, your secretary, and your child's teacher), indiscriminate dating, sex, dressing like the town tart—anything and everything may happen in an attempt to assure yourself that you're still desirable.

Not only is this behavior destructive, but it distracts from your work at hand—the process of divorcing and mending. Until both are complete, a new, satisfying relationship is impossible. This is also an important time in your relationship with your children.

Ralph, a Hollywood screenwriter says, "Dating, or meeting someone new, never really entered my mind, truthfully. My main concern ever since my wife and I split up about a year ago has been the twins, our four-year-old boy and girl. We'd been married for six years. My concern over the children is so strong, it's like tunnel vision. I actually said to myself, I hope the kids will like the next person I pick. It was never—I hope I can find the next person, but that the next person I find is a nice person. All around me, friends and acquaintances keep throwing phone numbers of single women at me. I know I'll have a lot of choices when the time is right for me to take those chances, to start dating, I'll have plenty of people to pick from.

"Maybe my attitude is gender based, I don't know. Women might fear no one will want them because they have kids. I know people who say they'll never remarry because it was such a bad experience.

"The fact that I was already in my forties when I got married might have something to do with my priorities and attitude. I think a lot of it is also guilt. I don't want to fail my children as a father. This marriage didn't work out, and while I can't blame myself for that entirely, marriage is a fifty-fifty proposition, I have to work harder at being a father because my kids don't have that normal family structure.

"I've also told myself that I'm worrying too much; after all, it's been a year and the kids seem fine. I have my own life to live, and there's more to life than just my work and my kids. I tell myself to get on with my life—I can't do this for the rest of my life. I'm not even sure why I'm so sensitive when it comes to the kids and dating. I guess I'm afraid they might feel displaced or something.

"Maybe it's been long enough. The funny thing is that kids at four years old already understand the concept of dating, probably from watching television."

Unfortunately, feeling confused during this time is normal. However, as an adult, you're still responsible for the way in which you act on this confusion.

## Suggestions

*Do* make the decision to separate or stay together—together. Even if you don't agree.

*Don't* suddenly disappear or pretend that the idea to leave was one you had just yesterday.

*Don't* use fear, or anger, as an excuse to justify behavior you know you'll later regret.

# CHAPTER THREE

## *The Moment of Truth*

*Tension beyond belief—something has to give. Who's
pretending anyway?*

"At 11 p.m. we finally started to talk about us," says Steve. "She
was bitter and spiteful. She didn't want me, so I asked her what she
was taking with her. We said good-bye for three hours. We spent our
last night together, but I never went to sleep. I held her and told her
how much I loved her and that I always would.

"When I left on Sunday to go to my mother's house with some
personal things, I hugged her and cried. A three-year chapter in my
life is gone, and I don't know what to do right now, this evening, or
for the rest of my life. I think about what she might be doing—and
how it's none of my business. I wanted to call her even last night, but
I know I can't. She wants to be friends, but I don't think I can look
her in the eyes without falling to pieces. She says she loves
me . . . well, you know. I think about her and then force myself to
remember the reality of the situation. I am really sad. I need to move
on and am wondering if there's a way to just ignore these painful
feelings."

You are stuck in time, unable to move forward, yet you can't live
in the past. The time has come for action—time to move along—almost in spite of yourself.

Rebecca remembers, "After living with asthma for a year, hating myself for being unable to bring my marriage to the end it deserved, one Wednesday (I remember it was a Wednesday), I woke, turned to my husband, and gasped in a rush of words, 'I can't do this anymore. I can't be married to you. You have to be out in two weeks. That's just the way it is.' He said, 'Is this because I forgot to give you your phone messages yesterday?' Finally and absolutely, I was speechless."

Claire, a Los Angeles artist recalls, "I remember sitting at the kitchen bar with my husband, also an artist, *that* morning. Although the subject of my leaving had been in the air for a while, we finally began to talk about it in concrete terms. With such sadness, he said he didn't want me to go, he wouldn't be able to live without me. I said that I have to go, we don't get along. I can't see a future for my-self with you. I knew that as long as I stayed in that marriage, I had no tomorrow."

At that time, Claire and her husband were living in an area of the city that wasn't far from the place they'd lived when they were first married, about sixteen years before. "Suddenly," says Claire, "he stood and with this great air of regret, said he had to walk over to our 'old house.' I walked with him. Looking at that tiny house, the two of us stood, remembering—each in our own way—a very dif-ferent, happy time in our lives. When we finally walked home, he was extremely, extremely sad."

For some, this moment of truth is a long time in coming, but for others, it's a moment of truth that comes without warning, a moment that abruptly changes your life forever. Erica, a mother of two, says, "I was married for eighteen years and had two daughters who were twelve and eight at the time of my divorce. My own background in-cludes alcoholic parents and a stepfather. Looking back, it's pretty obvious that all I had wanted was someone who would love me, I was looking for a father. My husband was twenty-two years older than me and from another country, another culture."

Erica and her husband had dated for four years before she mar-ried him. During their marriage, they fought over the children he had from his first marriage, children, although grown and older than

Erica, who seemed to always come first in his life. They still lived in the country he'd come from. But life went on.

"One morning, to my horror, my twelve-year-old daughter told me she had been sexually molested by her father. I confronted him, and although he denied it at first, he finally admitted it. I called child-protective services, but they would only come out and talk to us. I called the police, even though I was afraid he would kill us or take the children and run to another country.

"My mom had also called that morning. When I told her what had happened, she told me about a woman's shelter. The children and I went to the shelter that night. Leaving was a very hard thing to do, but I felt I had no choice. Because I pressed charges against my husband, while it was being investigated, my children were taken away from me for what turned out to be seventy-two hours. We eventually stayed in the shelter for nine weeks."

## Suggestions

*Do* keep in mind this is probably one of the scariest moments of your life, but once you have successfully navigated through it, your energies can be redirected into rebuilding your life in a positive direction.

# CHAPTER FOUR

## *Relief–Euphoria–Terror*

*You told and didn't die. You're in control again. Life is good. But now you really do have to leave.*

Will I be happier? Should I really be doing this? What day of the week is it? You've told your spouse, you weren't struck dead by lightning, but now you really do have to leave. Or do you? Second thoughts are part of trying to figure out if you're doing the right thing. This is not an easy question to answer.

You're sure you've thought about it to death, even before telling your spouse. But now, deciding simply whether you would be happier without your spouse shifts to seriously considering what your alternatives might be as a single person. While some people might prefer to stay single after divorce, most think about their chances for remarriage.

One reality, according to national surveys over the past two decades, is that divorced and separated people are more negative and have lower levels of (life) satisfaction than married people. Divorced people also have poorer physical health and are more often depressed.

According to 6,573 respondents to a 1987-88 National Survey of Families and Households, (even though factors such as income and education were more important) people in first marriages reported

greater happiness and less depression than those who had ever divorced. And, going one step further, people who had divorced just
once were less depressed than those with a history of two or more
divorces. Those currently married reported greater happiness and
less depression than cohabiters, who in turn reported greater well-
being on those two scores than those who lived without another
adult.

Could this mean that people who divorce are more inclined to be
unhappy people regardless of their marital situation? Counselors
suggest that in some cases, you might be happier trying to improve
your relationship than divorcing. Is it possible that wanting a divorce
is your way of trying to solve a personal problem? If so, blaming
your spouse and getting a divorce won't help unless you take a good
look at, and learn to manage, your personal problems as well.

A healthy marriage offers emotional support, sexual gratification,
companionship, and economic and practical benefits. Unhappy
marriages don't. Compared with *unhappily* married people, people
who are divorced generally enjoy better physical and emotional
health and a more positive attitude. In short, while a healthy marriage can have a strong positive effect on your well-being, the reverse
is also true in a troubled marriage.

The bottom line? Will a divorce be a step away from a relationship
that cannot be improved, or is it an illusory way to solve personal
problems? Confused? A marriage counselor may help you understand your motives and the consequences of divorce.

Divorce counseling, where you and your partner learn to negotiate conflicts, can be a lifesaver when it comes to avoiding an all-out
war. The goal is to help you accept and adjust to the divorce so that
eventually you can turn what is now a crisis into an opportunity for
learning and personal growth. A divorce counselor can also help you
to cope with feelings of hostility brought on by the legal arrangements that are part of divorce and help you help your children adjust to their loss.

Feelings of ambivalence and vacillation aren't uncommon. Does
this mean you might not be ready for divorce? Try to balance all of
the anticipated moral, social, economic, and familial consequences

against your current satisfactions, insecurities, and unhappiness. Weighing alternatives, you will go through periods of agonizing indecision. Parting is a long process, as you gradually redefine yourself, and your spouse, as single.

Once you decide that you definitely want the divorce, you might be surprised by a sense of urgency, a need to act quickly to satisfy your needs. Marriage counselors advise against making quick decisions, especially if you're motivated by feelings of hate or anger. You might find it helpful to try a period of structured separation, i.e. living apart for a limited time before getting involved with lawyers or new relationships, while you continue counseling together.

Readiness for divorce is not only in the wanting but a willingness to take responsibility for your contribution to the breakup. It also means feeling comfortable with the decision over a reasonable period of time, without extreme vacillation.

You may not want, or be ready, to end your marriage. It may have been your spouse's choice. Regardless of who does the leaving, divorce and its aftermath can be unexpectedly traumatic.

## Suggestions

*Do* look at your contribution to your problems and the breakup of this marriage as honestly as you can.

*Don't* be surprised by second thoughts about leaving. Have trust in your inner voice.

*Do* be aware that keeping the marriage intact may be a far better solution than divorce if you, and your spouse, are willing to realistically acknowledge your individual problems and seek answers not only individually but together as a couple.

# CHAPTER FIVE

## *The Leaver and the Left*

*Yes, it does make a difference. It's called self-esteem.*

*-and-*

## *Crime and Punishment/Support Withdrawal*

*What uncle's ninetieth party did you say you'd attend with your spouse? Had a bad day at the office, honey? Tough. Had a fender bender on the way home? Oh, well.*

Not surprisingly, research shows that the degree of trauma you suffer usually depends on whether you or your spouse wanted the dissolution, at least partly because the one feeling "left" experiences a greater loss of control. It's perfectly natural to feel awful when you're rejected and discarded. It makes an enormous difference emotionally (in both your reaction and recovery) whether you are the one who actively sought the divorce or the one who accepted or fought it.

The announcement "I want a divorce" might have come as a total surprise which, understandably, pulled the emotional rug out from under you. When this happens, you feel abandonment, the initiator feels guilt; you feel helpless, they feel in control; you feel fear that's in line with their anger and loss where they feel resentment. He or she has already spent time on feelings, strategies, and justifications while you're caught totally unsuspecting and unprepared.

The breakup of a very short marriage can be as difficult an experience as a marriage that's lasted for years. Even though Hank had been married for only four months when his wife told him she thought of him only as a friend, he was devastated. "She said," adds Hank, "that she no longer had any romantic feelings toward me and was leaving.

"I come from a stable family, hers was a very dysfunctional one, but we'd known each other for two years before walking down the aisle. When I said 'I do' I meant it—I was going to spend the rest of my life with this woman. I am not one who gives up easily, but this feels out of control. I can't force her to stay with me, that would make her miserable and in turn hurt me.

"We have decided to go to counseling, but the more I talk to her, the more I think she's already made up her mind. I can't seem to keep my feelings under control anymore. My eyes water at work, I'm not concentrating on my job. I feel completely helpless."

Shaun's separation, after an eight-year marriage, left him reeling. Remembering the sequence of events, he recalls, "My wife told me that the marriage was not working for her and that she wanted to separate. She said that she no longer felt any love for me and hadn't for some time. My heart was broken. I loved her so much. We have two children, and my family was my life. I was scared of losing them all. I was also angry and hurt.

"The evening before my wife and two daughters packed up and moved several thousand miles away, I went to say good-bye to the girls. I had hoped that they would be obnoxious or something, but they weren't. They were absolutely adorable. When I started to cry, my oldest smiled and said, 'Daddy, you're crying aren't you?' I said yes, and she replied, 'That's okay, I'm not going to be upset . . . I promise.' God, I love those kids. Unfortunately, I love Sharon, too. I hope that with time, I can learn not to love her anymore. I'm finding out that what keeps a couple together is compatibility and shared interests, not love. Love simply makes incompatibility painful.

"Now, I am truly alone for the first time in my life. I substituted Sharon for my parents, and now she is gone. Not even in the same town or state. As hard as it is, I must try to find a way of rebuilding my self-esteem. God, this is going to be hard. Though I know I have some good points, I really don't like myself very much. I wish I could find someone to love me, but I'm not sure I would believe them if they did."

Shaun even found himself sitting on the sofa with photos of his family spread on the coffee table, a loaded handgun in his mouth. Fortunately, he called a suicide-prevention line and talked with them for more than an hour and a half. "I am so grateful to them for being there."

He spent a lot of time with his daughters over the Easter holiday. He talked to his ex-wife. Naturally, he was pretty upset to learn that she had become intimate with his best friend. They talked about her relationship with the friend, and Shaun discovered that, indeed, she was in love with him. "It hurt me but helped me to find some closure with her," says Shaun.

"I decided to begin dating. And I have done so without prejudice. In a matter of months, I've dated more than all my years prior to meeting Sharon. It is grueling, but I am learning a great deal about myself. It's what I need to do at this point. I should have learned these social skills long ago."

His children came to live with him for the summer. He was sure that once they were with him, his feelings of self-pity, anger, regret, fear, and loneliness would be gone, at least temporarily. Not so. "I've tried to do things to get over this self-hatred I'm feeling. I have, rightly, lost much weight. I have asked countless women out. I joined an expensive dating service, which proved to be the biggest waste of money I've ever spent. Most of the women in the service were fat, ugly, husband-seeking psychos. Those that weren't, were definitely not interested in fat, ugly, recently divorced men. Bummer. I shaved off my goatee and cut off my ponytail. I even bought a new car. Nothing helped. I still loved Sharon dearly."

Sometimes Shaun wonders if he'll always be alone. "Or, I wonder, if indeed, there might be someone out there who is perfect for me and I for her. Pipe dreams? I can't help but think about them. I'm jealous that my wife is now in love with my best friend. I suppose it's normal to be jealous about that. But I have another jealousy that is just sickening. I am actually jealous of Sharon, as well as Tom. It makes me angry that she is doing so well while I am not!

"The other issue is that I wonder just how all this is affecting the girls. They seem to be doing extremely well. I wonder if it wouldn't be better for me to just stay out of their lives, to let Bill become a sort of surrogate father to them."

Caring for his daughters over the summer was difficult at first. Imagine having a full-time job while being responsible for their care, with no family around to take the edge off. "It was really hard at first, but then things became easier as we fell into a routine. I'd drop them off at day care every morning at 8:30 and head for work. Then, most days, I'd pick them up for lunch. At 5:30, we'd head out to run errands and go home. Supper, baths, hair washing, and before I knew it, it was 9:30 and time for bed. While they slept, I'd do laundry and clean up the kitchen.

"Once I called Sharon to ask her something, and Tom had apparently changed the message on the machine to say '. . . Sharon and I aren't in right now . . .' Guess I won't be calling there anymore.

"I found myself thinking that once the girls left, I could, for the most part, do what I wanted. My only restriction was being stuck in my job. I'd love to try acting, or comedy, or something different. But I have to pay a child-support figure that is based on my current salary."

A month later, Shaun feels "bizarre." "I don't feel like I'm living my life. Rather, I'm watching it happen. I react to things as I normally would, then some part of me analyzes what has happened and passes judgment on me. I don't like or admire myself much. I'm not the kind of person that I'd want to model my life after. I'm not psychotic. I realize it's just that I am filled with such self-hatred and loathing.

"Frankly, it didn't seem fair. Here was a person that I couldn't stand, and I was forced to live with him for the rest of my life. I simply had no choice and didn't know what to do about it. My entire life I've been a problem solver. I'd identify problems and search for ways to fix them. But this was a problem that I couldn't find a solution for. In spite of the fact that the girls were here with me, and we were doing fine—they even seemed to be enjoying themselves—I still felt totally empty and useless. I'd look in the mirror and see a person that I didn't like one bit. I wanted a new me."

But that's not the way life works. We can't just say, "Aww, I think I'll get myself a different personality, a different body, and a different history." Shaun admits he has no desire to talk to any of his friends. He doesn't care what they're doing. His mother and father call often, trying to be chipper and upbeat. "They always end the conversation with 'I love you,' as if they're waiting for me to respond in kind. But I have a hard time doing so. I'm not sure that I even care about them. Yet, this uncaring attitude frightens me. Who could like a person that doesn't care about anyone?"

Looking for a new job, Shaun tries to get excited about something. It doesn't seem to be working. "Should I get an interview, I am not certain that I will even be able to fake excitement and enthusiasm."

A week later, Shaun and his daughters are invited by a woman he's dated a few times to spend the day together. "My ineptitude with relationships really hit home to me then." His disbelief that anyone could really care for him, and his need to protect himself from rejection, kept him distant—the opposite of what she appeared to want.

"You see, these were the same problems I had at the time that I met Sharon. Fortunately, she didn't wait around for me to get over the fear. She just attacked me, sexually. But I wonder if my feelings for Sharon aren't at least adding to my hesitation. Is it possible that, at least on some level, I still feel married? Certainly, that would be foolish, considering Sharon's current situation. But maybe that, too, is playing a part in how I'm feeling."

Three months go by, and Shaun is beginning to see a light at the end of the tunnel. "Up until yesterday," says Shaun, "I felt terrible. While it was wonderful spending the summer with my daughters, I became quite lonely for my wife. I felt a continuing need to hang on to what no longer existed.

"Yesterday, however, my divorce became final. And, strangely enough, that afternoon I started to feel better. Perhaps yesterday was the beginning of my new life. While my self-esteem is quite low, I am hopeful that someday I, too, will find someone special . . . as my wife has done."

After nearly eight years of marriage, Allison's husband told her that he is planning to leave. "I feel like it is my fault," says Allison, "but he keeps telling me it isn't. Both of us cry constantly, neither of us can eat, sleep, or function. He says he didn't want this to happen, but our marriage hasn't been that great, I guess. Not bad, just not good, either.

"We've recently bought a new house. We have a six-year-old son and a year-old daughter. Everything seemed to be going well. Sex was minimal, we argued a lot and were often sarcastic to one another—basically that's our personalities. He now says that he is very unhappy and doesn't have it in him to try anymore. I keep telling him that we can make an honest effort to fix things, but he says he just can't.

"He has been staying at his mom's while she is on vacation and has been gone a week. He says he will come back tomorrow night, and we will talk more then. I am really scared. We married young, in our early twenties, and dated for several years before that. I thought we would be married forever and can't imagine life without him.

"I don't want to be an ex-wife, a divorcée. I don't want my kids to live like that. The custody, the separations, etc. I can't stop crying. I just started a new job with a good salary and benefits, our life should have been looking up for us. I have more to lose than he does. He's smart, funny, good looking, a hard worker, fun to be with, sexy, and very sweet. He is also a very good cook! I can't believe this is happening to me."

Does it surprise you that retaliation might be in the heart and minds of some? Crime and punishment—the withdrawal of emotional support. It goes something like: *What uncle's ninetieth party did you say I said I'd attend? Had a bad day at the office, honey? Tough. A fender bender on the way home? Oh, well.*

Emotionally, divorce involves not only withholding communication and the emotions which once bonded you and yours, but typically, you begin to replace these positive feelings with ones of alienation. These new feelings can't help but show up in the way you treat your soon-to-be ex. Instead of reinforcing, you begin to undermine their self-esteem with endless large and small betrayals: responding with blame rather than comfort to a spouse's disastrous day, for instance, or refusing to go to a party given by their family, friends, or colleagues. As emotions intensify, betrayals become greater.

Regardless of the particular circumstances of your failing marriage, both of you feel profoundly disappointed, misunderstood, and rejected. Because your partner's very existence is a symbol of failure and rejection, you continually grate on each other. One of you may even want the marriage held together for any number of reasons—continued attachment, fear of being alone, what's best for the children, the determination to be faithful to marriage vows—yet you continue to hurt one another as you communicate your frustration with just the look on your face, your posture, and the tone of your voice.

Letting your partner hear your frustration and anger with words (at the appropriate times, minus an audience) can help to defuse your anger and the negative feelings you're having about yourself. No matter what's going on around you, value your behavior and your ability to be direct and honest.

## Suggestions

*Don't* be impatient with yourself. Divorce is an emotional process which embraces many moods and feelings.

*Don't* be surprised at the depth of rage you might be feeling. It's okay to give your feelings a voice—just pick your time, place, and to whom. You want to feel better for airing your feelings, not worse.

# CHAPTER SIX

## *Shock*

*Never, ever in a hundred million years did you consider
the possibility that this could be happening to you.*

At forty, Noemi, mother of two, fully expected her marriage to last
a lifetime. Despite the normal ups and downs of every marriage, she,
in fact, had no reason to suspect otherwise.

"Sam and I met when I was nine years old, he was eleven," recalls
Noemi. "At that time, he had gone to live with his foster mother—
my mother's best friend. Many years later I was to learn that his foster mother treated him badly, without any real love or caring."

Over the years, Noemi's family stayed in touch through family
gatherings, including her sweet sixteen party. Her father died when
she was eighteen, and Sam came to the funeral. That year Sam joined
the military, and she went to college in her home state, California.
He enrolled in the same college after he was discharged. Noemi attended days, Sam went nights.

"One day I answered the phone when his foster mother called.
Naturally the conversation turned to Sam. I discovered we were
going to the same school, we even had a class in common—just at
different times. He called needing a paper, and we talked for over
three hours. He asked me out, and although I'd been dating someone quite seriously for about two-and-a-half years, I went. Four

weeks later, we were married. We were a perfect match, I needed someone that I could care for and he was it. Everyone begged us not to get married, thinking it was too quick, but we weren't about to listen to anyone. My mother in particular. She felt that I was getting into a real mess because both of his natural parents had committed suicide, when he was five and eleven.

"I dropped out of school because that was what he wanted, although he would deny that today. He went on and graduated. At that point, we moved to New York. I would have preferred to stay in California, but one trip east and his mind was made up. We wanted to start a family, and eighteen months later, I became pregnant."

Their marriage was fine until they had children. "Maybe things changed because there wasn't as much of me to go around. He was fine when the baby was little, but by the time he was four, the tension mounted. I remember when I got pregnant, he was so excited when the test finally came back positive. It was a very easy pregnancy but a rough delivery. In fact, he passed out in the delivery room. But he was thrilled to have a child. Before the children, we enjoyed being together, even though we didn't have much money and life was hard. We did a little traveling, went to a movie now and then, we were with friends a lot."

Noemi's mother moved with them to New York because she'd sold her house. Sam and she soon had a fight, and he threw her out of their apartment. "He had a very bad temper—he still does—and he wouldn't talk to her for years. But, despite the ups and downs, my marriage was solid. He wasn't as romantic as I had hoped, but we had a nice marriage.

"When our first child was about twelve, my mom became ill. She had to have surgery, and he refused to pay for it. You see, I had been paying her a salary for a couple of years. I'd gone into the catering business. I had tons of equipment and supported all kinds of staff— he said it cost him a fortune and never made money. I don't know, I didn't do the books. However, I think the real issue was that he wanted me home, twenty-four hours a day, at his beck and call. So I'd be in the kitchen cooking all day long and then, for example, he'd be angry if I didn't want to cook dinner. I was tired but he wouldn't understand.

"Our marriage didn't fall apart. In retrospect, I think he just got to the point when he needed something else in his life. He didn't know what he needed, just something else. I don't know if he knows it today. After our second child was born, I sensed he was looking, but he never had affairs that I know of. There was a woman in his professional practice that he went to bat for, making her a partner when no one else thought it appropriate. And then, he fired her because she wasn't any good. I don't think he had an affair with her, it was more that he doesn't like to be wrong about anything, and it bothered him no end to be wrong."

When their second child came, the first was about four and a half, and Sam was already having trouble—he was about that age when his mother had committed suicide. By the time their first child was eleven, Sam couldn't take it—he couldn't be close to either one. "I don't think he even knew what was going on," recalls Noemi. "He tried *not* to be involved, he tried to *be* involved. He just didn't know where he fit in. We fought and I considered leaving him—I was angry at him, I suppose. But I'm the type that commits to something and I stay, no matter what."

Noemi asked Sam to go to counseling and finally, he said he would after refusing for years. What she didn't know at the time was that he had already made up his mind to leave—he'd already rented an apartment. "I wasn't allowed to participate in the emotional process of his leaving. I was told after he'd make up *his* mind—after he already had a new relationship.

"When he told me he was leaving, but not about living with a woman, I was absolutely shocked. He even asked me to go shopping with him to stock his apartment with appliances, etc. He'd never gone alone. So, stupid me, I went. A week later, I telephoned his apartment and a woman answered. I said, 'Is Sam there?' She said, 'No.' I said, 'Who's this?' And, she said, 'This is Kay.' I said, 'Excuse me!? Is he coming back?' And she said, 'Yes, I'll leave him a message.' A half hour later, my phone rang and he said, 'I guess you're angry.' Truthfully I wasn't. At that point all I could feel was hurt, it took my breath away. He asked if I wanted him to tell me about her. I knew who she was, that's what had hurt the most. She had worked for a company where I'd worked for many years—in fact, that's how he'd met her. What he didn't tell me was that they were living together, he'd moved in with her right out of our home. When he left, he simply gave me his new phone number.

"Soon after, our younger child asked to visit his father's place, having never seen it. When my son came home, he said he had to talk to me. He said, 'Well, Dad's got a new apartment.' I said, 'Yes, I know.' 'It's got a pool table.' And I said, 'Yes, I know.' 'It's got a hot tub.' I said, 'Yes, I know.' 'And it's got a woman that he lives with. Did you know?' I said, 'Yes.' 'How long have you known?' I said, 'It doesn't matter.' But I *didn't* know. I had to learn about it from my thirteen-year-old son.

"Today, years later, I'm still hurting. It's hard to talk about. I just signed the final divorce papers. I just can't see the divorce the way he sees it. Sam thinks it's a wonderful opportunity for me! He's never done anything without a plan. He didn't leave his marriage until he had another relationship and life in place. I, on the other hand, only got married once and never intend to get married again. I wouldn't go through this again. In our support agreement, if I were to live with somebody for two years, he'll consider me *married,* so therefore, by his definition, I consider him remarried because he's been living with her for two years. If I could make a wish and have my life happy again, I know the answer wouldn't be a new someone, it would be some*thing.* I need to be busy, to feel like I'm accomplishing something."

John, married for more than nineteen years, a father of two, reminds us that this kind of shock happens to men as well as women. It's not gender based.

"I met Laura," says John, "when she was seventeen, I was twenty-four. We were married less than two years later and lived in the suburbs of Chicago. I worked for a large national consumer company, and she worked for an import company as a clerk."

Their first daughter was born in 1979, and Laura quit work to care for the child full time. Later that year, John was promoted and transferred to Kalamazoo, Michigan. Their second daughter was born in early 1981. Two years later, John was transferred again, to Champaign, Illinois. They stayed there for four years until he was transferred to another division in Kentucky, which included a large salary increase. "My wife took a job working as a newspaper carrier for the *Kentucky Star,* a very lucrative job. It was also a great job because she was still able to be home in the mornings and after school for the kids.

"In November of that year, she decided we needed a bigger house, so we bought a wonderful house, double the value of our old one. She said it was the house she'd always wanted."

At first, their problems had to do with work. "I resigned from my job after nineteen years with full severance because things were not working out. We honestly thought that with my background and experience finding a new job would be easy. We decided to stay put geographically, which limited my job search. Six months later, and still no job, my frustration began coming out in anger. She took over the management of another paper route to get us through financially after my severance ran out.

"I began working for her. She wasn't a good boss, and our arguments grew, or my anger grew while my self-esteem and self-worth plummeted. She told me how unhappy she was, but in very vague terms. I was also unhappy, and so I thought we were just going through a rough time in our lives and marriage."

In early August, Laura made a visit to see her parents and a good friend. John had no idea that the purpose of this trip was to tell them she'd made a decision to leave him. When she returned, and with much probing, she told him she thought they should separate. "She blamed it on all kinds of things—not enough friends, not enough sex, fighting with our daughters, my not being supportive of her job. All this came straight out of the blue as far as I was concerned."

They already had a vacation scheduled and paid for, a trip to the Ozarks to visit with Laura's sister's family, so they went. "It was wonderful, we acted like newlyweds—making love every chance we could get. I thought things would be okay. Things were great for a few days after we got home, and then she asked why I was being like that. I said, 'Because I love you and do not want a divorce. I thought that this was one of the things you wanted more of.' She accused me of faking it. I was in a lose/lose situation.

"We tried living separate lives, in one house, and went to counseling. She went twice and announced that I was the sick one—she would not go anymore. We both needed to take antidepressants just to function. A short time later, she announced that we needed to separate, i.e. live in different houses. I went into a thirteen-hour tirade of fear and depression. I pleaded, begged, yelled, screamed, and swore at her. The kids were there for about half of it. We finally collapsed in exhaustion."

The next day John came home from an errand and found Laura in tears, hysterical. "She told me to move and drove away in her car. I grabbed some things and went to a hotel. Remember, I'm still working for her, seeing her most every night delivering papers. I tried everything I could to make sense of the situation. I talked with her mother and sister but nothing seemed to help matters.

"I saw a lawyer but decided that filing would only push things in a direction I didn't want it to go. Then she told me she'd already filed. Our divorce was final sixty-five days later. During the separation, we argued, held each other—just to get through it. She kept sending mixed signals, saying she loved me, spending time with me, but, she would not stop the divorce action.

"I finally got a job but had a difficult time concentrating on it. I didn't do a good job. The kids wouldn't talk to me. My life was so tedious and hard and filled with difficult emotions. Three days after our divorce, I saw her with another man. She wouldn't tell me who it was, saying that not telling was part of her new boundaries for me. We still struggled with things such as medical bills, credit cards, all kinds of financial issues that the divorce did not solve.

"She made plans to move back to the Chicago area, to a small town 'for the kids.' I said that before she left, we owed it to ourselves and the girls to try at least one more time. We went out and had a good time. Two days later, she told me she was definitely moving in March. She was in love with someone, and the girls were going with her. I asked about the guy, since my daughters

would be living with him. It turned out to be the guy she was dat-
ing when I bumped into her, the one she'd refused to talk about.
He is also divorced, with two teenage boys and living outside of
Milwaukee."

Laura sold their house and found a townhome. The youngest
daughter decided to live with John. The eldest, after two weeks, decided also to live with John. "So, eight months after the divorce, she's
happily living with this guy and his two sons. My daughters are
angry at her for 'abandoning' them and angry at me about the divorce. I recently lost my job and am in a national job search looking
for another.

"I'm having trouble getting over Laura and feel badly about the
kids. I date but am not ready for a committed relationship. I am trying to build a life out of the ashes for myself and my daughters. It's
a hard road!"

Noemi and John were left with a difficult emotional job—having
to distance themselves from a spouse they were still in love with. A
painful recovery process which has at least three stages. Your first reaction is shock and denial. Eventually, the facts cannot be ignored—
you know you can't go on that way.

Reality sets in, and the second stage brings anger and depression,
coupled with confusion. You might even miss and hate your partner
at the same time.

Emotional wounds need time to close. The book *How to Survive
the Loss of a Love: 58 Things to Do When There Is Nothing to Be Done*
suggests some ways to facilitate the healing process while in this second stage. In a nutshell, they are:

1. Do your mourning *now*. Everything else can wait. The sooner
   you allow yourself to be with your pain, the sooner it will pass.
   Resisting the mourning only postpones healing, and grief can return months or even years later to haunt you.
2. Be gentle with yourself. Accept that you have an emotional
   wound, that it is disabling, and that it will take a while before
   you are completely well. Treat yourself with the same consideration you would offer a friend in a similar situation.

3. If possible, don't take on new responsibilities. When appropriate, let employers and coworkers know you're healing.

4. Don't blame yourself for any mistakes (real or imagined) that brought you to this loss. You can acknowledge mistakes later, when the healing process is further along.

5. Remember that it's okay to feel depressed. A time of convalescence is important. Just follow your daily routine and let yourself heal.

6. For a while, don't get involved in a passionate romance or a new project that requires great time and energy.

7. Don't try against obvious odds to rekindle the old relationship. Futile attempts at reconciliation are painful and a waste of recuperative energy.

8. If you find photographs and mementos helpful to the mourning process, use them. If you find they bind you to a dead past, get rid of them. Put them in the attic, sell them, give them away, or throw them out.

9. Remember that it's okay to feel anger toward God, society, or the person who left you. But it is *not* okay or good for you to hate yourself or to act on your anger in a destructive way. Let the anger out safely: hit a pillow, kick the bed, sob, scream (when the kids aren't within seeing or hearing distance). Practice screaming as loudly as you can. A car with the windows up makes a great scream chamber.

10. Use addictive prescription drugs like Valium wisely. Take them only if prescribed by your physician and only for a short period of time. *Don't* take them to mask your grief.

11. Watch your nutrition. Take vitamins, eat good foods, and try to get plenty of rest.

12. Don't overindulge in alcohol, marijuana or other recreational chemicals, or cigarettes.

13. Pamper yourself a little. Get a manicure, take a trip, bask in the sun, sleep late, see a good movie, visit a museum, listen to music, take a long bath instead of a quick shower. As time progresses, remember that it's okay *not* to feel depressed.

14. You might find keeping a journal or diary helpful. This way you can see your progress as you read past entries.
15. Go at your own pace. The sadness comes and goes—though it comes less frequently and for shorter lengths of time as healing proceeds.

In the third stage, you are ready to take a look at your part and admit some responsibility in the failure of the relationship. Along with this clarity, you can begin to forgive yourself and your mate and get on with your life. As long as you see your ex-spouse as the enemy—or are still seething—you're still tied in emotionally. Preoccupation with your ex-spouse, along with bitterness and hatred, are the emotions of a continuing relationship. Counseling can help. Community and religious groups offer workshops that can also be very beneficial because of their group environment.

## Suggestions

*Do* take care of yourself by eating a healthy diet, exercising, and getting the emotional support you need.

# CHAPTER SEVEN

## *Social Obligations*
*Are you or aren't you a couple?*

"My husband and I are in the process of splitting up, but we haven't filed the papers yet because we want to get our debts paid off," says Betty. Sounds logical, but where does this leave you as a couple—and, what about your feelings? Betty claims that she is "fine with most of how things are going with this arrangement, we're pretty much living our separate lives."

Is there a problem? "He's taking HER to his company picnic. We both agreed that we're free to date other people, and I can see whomever I want, whenever I want, and do just about anything I feel like doing. But I just can't stand the idea that he's seeing HER, the woman he needed so much more than me that he was willing to sacrifice our marriage over it.

"It's not like things would magically be wonderful again for us even if he were to suddenly decide to give her up—his relationship with her is more a symptom of what was wrong with our marriage, not the cause of it. I don't even want a reconciliation with him at this point. Nevertheless, it would make me very, very happy if she were to suddenly shrivel up and drop off the face of the earth.

"Hate is a destructive emotion, I know, but I can't figure out how to be a calm, rational adult human being when it comes to this woman. I stood by this man through all of his ups and downs, and now that he's finally okay, she's getting the new man I helped him to become.

"Maybe it will be less confusing once we're legally separated, that way I won't be caught between my old and new lives."

Tony's experience is, in some ways, similar. "When my ex and I started to talk about separating, we both said, 'Oh, we're mature adults—we'll just live together until we get our feet on the ground.' We were both students at that time. 'We'll be like roommates.' Neither of us dated, which was a good thing because the situation was difficult without adding jealousy to the mix. She used her newfound freedom to establish a social life, and I was using mine to write exams. But I was angry all the time, both at myself and at her, and I felt incredibly confused.

"Looking back, I think I was using the anger and hatred to distance myself emotionally from her, something I couldn't do while still physically living with her."

## Suggestions

*Do* know there is a time of feeling absolutely confused about the day-to-day mechanics of your life. You are about to learn a new way of living.

*Do* allow yourself to take it one day at a time and to deal with each situation as it comes up. It is impossible to know how you will be feeling next week, much less an hour from now.

*Don't* rush into action. Allow yourself to handle each situation according to what is appropriate right now, not a month ago, or what you think you will be feeling a month from now. Give yourself the luxury of time, time you need to think before acting.

# CHAPTER EIGHT

## *Sexual Availability*
*You're still having sex with who!?*

Robin had sex with her ex-spouse several times after they were split up while they were going through divorce proceedings and then even after they were officially divorced—once. "The two times were for different reasons entirely," says Robin.

"Before we were actually divorced, we split up and got back together several times. It was difficult, to say the least, for me to finally make the decision to leave for good. I never could resist him physically, and I think I mistook incredible physical attraction and great sex for a good relationship. So I guess I kept having sex with him, and going back to him, out of my own weakness.

"The last time we had sex, on the other hand, was out of strength, I believe. I had finally made the break, I hadn't even seen him in a year. I felt I was no longer susceptible to him, but I had to make sure. So I saw him, and I slept with him, and I didn't feel anything. Not even regret. I was just relieved to know it was finally over."

"We gave it a shot after we got separated," recalls Stewart. "It was more her idea than mine, she sort of initiated it. I went along with it, on a why-not basis. It was an equitable divorce. We only did it once because I started dating my current wife."

Katherine also continued to have sex with her husband after they separated, beginning about a month after he moved out. "I probably slept with him three or four times, which I initiated," says Katherine. "I did it because I'm the type of person who can't disconnect suddenly, regardless of the circumstances. I have to wean myself out of a situation gradually, and so I slept with him in order to get used to being without him. I also slept with him because I still harbored the hope that it would all work out."

When Katherine slept with him, he would spend the night. They used the children as an excuse to get together. "At that time my children were very young, three and seven. So when the kids would find daddy there the next day, of course, they were happy. I don't know if they were disappointed when he wouldn't show up again that night. At that point in my life, I was so engrossed with my own problems that I have to admit I don't remember noticing one way or another. It wasn't discussed.

"I began to realize that this relationship didn't and wasn't going to work for me, there was no way I could be happy with him. Another important factor was that I was involved in another relationship with a college professor. That relationship had been ongoing for a while. Having contact with both men gave me the opportunity to realize more and more how different I felt with each man and that my marriage was not going to work. And so I was able to finally move on emotionally and stop having sex with my husband."

Continuing to have sex with your spouse isn't all that uncommon. Is it a problem?

Having sex with your spouse at this point interferes with your ability to separate, to say good-bye, and to let it end, according to Catherine Inglove, marriage-family-child counselor in private practice in West Los Angeles. And, in doing so, your pain is prolonged.

"A lot of people are really frightened of being alone, they're afraid of feeling that lonely, empty feeling," says Inglove. "To avoid that awful feeling of detachment, they try to stay connected—in whatever way they can. Both men and women mistake sexual intimacy for emotional intimacy. Given that people believe sex is always part of intimacy, it's a way to still feel valued, to feel that someone still likes you, still finds you attractive.

"In other words, if he or she still has sex with you, it means, you think, that he or she doesn't really hate me—reading a lot of emotional feelings into it that probably aren't there. So then, when the inevitable happens and reality sets in, there's the possibility of feeling doubly betrayed. When you keep giving of yourself, and then feel used, it can only add to your bitterness and anger.

"Surprisingly, when you're about to separate, it's not all that uncommon for sex to seem better for some reason. It's somewhat of a mystery to me. I've never been able to completely understand why this happens because sex should take on an empty feeling or just not feel as satisfying. There should be some kind of holding back when you know that you're going to get a divorce. But for some couples, a small percentage, sex is better than ever. Perhaps, for these men and women, an edge of desperation gives sex an intensity that's mistaken for passion. Or, perhaps these people are able to shut off their real feelings, their emotional pain, and allow themselves to experience only the physical passion. Perhaps.

"Gender may play some role in what motivates the continued sex. Women may do it more from the emotional place of not wanting to feel lonely or worthless. Men also have these feelings and will do it for those same reasons, but with less awareness. If a man has not found a girlfriend, or is not even dating, he might begin to have those same kinds of worthless feelings. However, he may not be tuned into his emotions, and so, he only feels the physical needs. After all, men do need to ejaculate, it is a physiological phenomenon. When semen and fluids build up, if they're not ejaculated, men begin to feel physical discomfort. Of course, masturbation is a simple solution to this physical need, but equally great may be the need to prove they're still a man. The thinking goes: If my soon-to-be exspouse wants to have sex with me, I'm still a desirable man.

"Another part of the mix is who's leaving whom. Where the man has left, or is leaving, because he has a new girlfriend, he's not likely to still be having sex with his ex. But when neither one has a new partner, they might engage in sex. If either partner has a new love in their life, you don't see that happening."

What about the children? How might they be affected? "Assuming that daddy has moved out of the house, or mommy depending on the particular situation," continues Inglove, "if the kids wake up in the morning to find daddy in the bedroom, they could easily get the idea that things are now okay, that daddy's come back. But then daddy gets up, showers, maybe has breakfast with the kids, and leaves. The children ask, 'Is daddy back?' Mom says, 'No.' They're confused, they don't understand what this means in their lives.

"Obviously this confusion is felt more by young children than by teenagers. But even teens still hope this means you're getting back together, that the family unit will be intact again. Kids hope that everything's been worked out when they find dad in mom's bed.

"If a couple had a history of conflict, even physical violence, teenagers might hate the idea that he's back. They dread that you may be getting back together. They finally have some peace with dad out of the house. So on top of all the feelings they're trying to sort out, mom's betrayal gets added to the mix. Keep in mind that we're talking about a very different kind of family unit, one that is like a war zone. Understandably those kids don't want dad back. There is a betrayal when he's back in the house, even if it's only over the weekend to be with mom.

"Even more than sex, I see couples use the children to stay tied to-gether long after it's appropriate or in anyone's best interest—'fami-lies' that continue to do things together as if they were still a family unit, still intact. They might have dad over for birthday celebrations, or the whole family gets together for Thanksgiving. I believe that families who choose to have dad and his girlfriend over for Thanks-giving, for example, are engaging in neurotic behavior. If asked, the ex-wife will say she's doing it because of the children, even when the children are grown. This is generally not so. More likely, she still hasn't come to grips with the rejection she felt when he wanted the divorce, she hasn't come to some kind of resolution within herself. Friends and family may even voice their disapproval, saying, 'How can you do that?' In the end, it doesn't matter what they may say. You'll still be doing it until you finally let go and don't need his or her validation anymore.

"When separated or divorced clients tell me they're still taking trips together, or birthdays, or Thanksgiving, etc., I talk to them about the confusion this creates in the children. Children need to have firm boundaries, to know that daddy, or the noncustodial parent, has his house and we have our house. We have our birthday parties here, at mommy's house, and then go to daddy's later on, or next week, for another birthday celebration. Christmas with mommy, and then Christmas with daddy, or whatever the arrangement is between the two parents.

"You're going to have to keep boundaries firm no matter how painful it is, because children can cope only if they know what's what. If they know that daddy is gone, they can begin to cope, but if he's in and out, in and out, they can't.

"While children need to know that mommy and daddy aren't hostile to one another, they can't function best with no boundaries or separateness at all."

## Suggestions

*Don't* continue to have sex with your spouse after you are separated—even if you're hoping for a reconciliation. You're only muddying the emotional waters, making necessary decisions more difficult.

*Don't* continue to have family holidays together *for the children.* This only creates confusion for the children and interferes with your ability to get on with your life.

*Do* honor and celebrate holidays and special occasions as a family, a new family.

# CHAPTER NINE

## *Emotional Accessibility*
*You want what!?*
*-and-*

## *Feeling Isolated*
*No one's gone through what you're going through or felt so alone.*

We know that Rebecca gave her husband two weeks notice to move out. What we don't know, but could certainly guess at, was the emotional climate in the home during those weeks. What must her feelings have been? Feelings can't remain in a suspended state. Did she pretend nothing had happened? Did she live with her husband as roommates, perhaps in a cold war?

"For the sake of the children," says Rebecca, "my husband and I managed to behave reasonably well. No awful fights—we tried to just go on. My biggest confusion during that difficult time was knowing my emotional boundaries. I wish I had known how to take care of my feelings while my world became more and more unstable."

"Rebecca was part of a couple," says Arthur Kovacs, Ph.D., a psychologist in private practice in Santa Monica, California, "that was able to manage great restraint and stability. I wish everybody were that mature. However, I wouldn't encourage any couple to do what Rebecca and her husband did. I think that once a decision is made, the separation should go forward, and the couple must move apart as quickly as possible.

"This needs to be done because it makes things clear not only for the couple but for the children, and it prevents that very ambiguity that Rebecca described. In some ways, all of us remain small children. We don't do well with ambiguity and uncertainty. We become anxious when the rules are unclear, when we don't know what's expected of us, and how we're to conduct ourselves."

Another common scenario. Your husband (or wife) is being unfaithful. You know it, have even been living with this knowledge for awhile. Although your relationship is seriously disintegrating, for a multitude of reasons you're not ready to bring the other's behavior into the open. How do you deal with the emotional ambiguity of this volatile situation? Even though you're not talking about the problem, you can bet it's there.

"Well, at least *one* person's living with the emotional ambiguity of it," suggests Dr. Kovacs. How do you create emotional boundaries, living in this kind of situation? "The answer is that you can't. The spouse trapped on this shifting sidewalk really needs a lot of support and caretaking. They must turn to *other* people, such as friends and relatives, or a psychotherapist. They need to get some wisdom and stability as they move forward and decide what to do with a partner who is causing such anguish."

In other words, it behooves you to stay emotionally available, but you have to redefine who's the right person, or people, to do this with. "That's right," says Dr. Kovacs, "and that's one of the anguishes of divorce. The very person who has been your primary support is becoming, at best, a stranger—or, at worst, a hateful enemy. You have to shift your needs—for intimacy and kindness, for understanding and support—to a new cast of characters as rapidly as possible."

Dr. Kovacs says if a separating couple in a long-term relationship doesn't have a good support system, one of the partners might appear seriously disturbed. "A mental health professional may then prescribe heavy doses of antipsychotic medication and to think about hospitalization. Fortunately, it's usually a transitory phase—it's like a terrible thunderstorm that runs its course.

"Within a brief time, the person will restabilize if there's no prior history of severe emotional disturbance. Friends and family who are a part of the 'new' support system should be supportive and not panicky. A person might be very disturbed for some period of time. They might weep uncontrollably, have temper tantrums, or threaten suicide, screaming that they can't stand it and they don't know what they're going to do—extremes of emotions in one way or another. Unfortunately it is not uncommon for children to witness these behaviors."

Your feelings of isolation are equally wrenching. You're sure that no one's ever gone through what you're going through or felt so alone.

John M. Haynes, in *Divorce Mediation,* has outlined twelve universal feelings that are all part of adjusting to what's going on in your life. They include rejection, anger, loneliness, confusion, self-doubt, depression, fear of making mistakes, fear of proving inadequate, fear of losing control, anxiety over the unknown, self-pity, and euphoria—not necessarily in that order.

The reason you might be feeling so alone is your need to isolate yourself from friends and family who, you feel, might judge what's happening to you as your failure. So you hide yourself and the truth to avoid, what you think, will compound your awful feelings.

You also might be hoping you'll work it out, and then there will be nothing to tell them. Why not save yourself all that embarrassment?

Instead, give your friends and family the chance to help. Don't hide your secret like dirty laundry. Being lovable has nothing to do with being perfect. That's *your* need, not theirs. Regardless of the particulars of your situation, there's a good chance they'll be there for you. No? You'll never know unless you give them the chance.

## Suggestions

*Do* avoid living with emotional ambiguity. Once a decision is made to separate, it should go forward as quickly as possible.

*Don't* allow yourself to shut down emotionally. Look to friends and family for nurturing and support.

# CHAPTER TEN

## *Attacks on Self-esteem*

*Going blonde, getting breast implants, buying a whole
new wardrobe. Getting hair implants, clothes that fit,
using cologne, pumping iron. Is it helping yet?*

Leslie and her husband had been married for seven years and together for six before that. "He decided last fall that 'he didn't want to
be married to me anymore,'" said Leslie. "He found someone to run
to, an old flame from fifteen years ago who happened to also be ending a marriage. I was in shock. His leaving came totally out of the
blue. We were having problems, no relationship is perfect, but I
didn't think things were that bad."

The week after he left, Leslie had her hair cut real short because
he'd never wanted her to have short hair. She bought a lot of new
clothes and jewelry. She also bought her first book on relationships
and marriage. Now she has about half a dozen around the house.
The books have helped her to realize it's all happened before, with
different names and faces. "In them," says Leslie, "I've found pieces
of him, myself, and our relationship. The books have helped me to
understand what I did wrong.

"I joined a support group. It was a relief to meet other people who
were going through a similar experience; I stopped feeling so alone.
I had always put his needs before mine. Basically my life revolved

around his. Finally I've started to gain control of my life. I went to Italy by myself—my first travel experience entirely alone; I started the legal separation; and I filed for divorce under grounds of adultery. I decided that I wouldn't be a victim anymore."

Leslie is now making decisions for herself, learning that she can depend on herself and that happiness can only truly come from within ourselves. "To my surprise, I've found someone I really like— myself. I have kept my dignity throughout this difficult time and intend to have a much happier life without him.

"Sure, I loved him very much. I still care. But the bottom line is that I care about myself more. I spent thirteen years of my youth with him. I gave up my desire to have children to be with him, which I now realize was wrong. My time is now for healing, not for taking care of him. I'm beginning to see that there is life after divorce and that I will have the last laugh."

Her attitude has made a world of difference. "I was a pessimist, now I'm an optimist. I've been dealt a bad set of cards, but I'm not about to let him ruin my life. He actually told me, twice, that he's sorry for ruining my life. Wrong! I'm the only one who can do that, and I no longer intend to."

Out of the misery of a difficult divorce, Leslie eventually came to have an enhanced sense of self-esteem—an improvement not just mentally but of her emotional and physical self as well. She began to move toward this awareness as she put her feelings of anxiety, guilt, and anger to positive use. "I started to apply skills and abilities which I didn't know I had to the new problems that came up with being single. The more I explored and tested the unfamiliar parts of myself, the more I integrated them into the notion of who I am."

Sophie recalls, "It took a long time for me to realize how much of myself I'd lost—how much I had become a mere extension of my husband. The depression and low self-esteem after we separated were horrible, and it felt as though it would never get better. It did. I eventually worked through it and was able to get on with my life. But it didn't happen overnight.

"During that time, I made an effort to find something fun to do with my life. Sometimes I had to consciously make myself take action. I made an effort to look good every day. I worked in the garden, got a job, even did volunteer work. Just like after a surgical operation, I needed time to heal. I went at my own pace, not what my friends thought it should have been. While they are well meaning, they aren't me.

"Four years later, I am here to tell you that the worst does pass. I resolved and found the wonderful me again. Tucked in my head is the thought that there is someone out there looking for me just the way I am. I finally came to realize that my ex wasn't so wonderful and stopped waiting for him to come back to me. Recovery is a day at a time. I know who I am now and am happy for my uniqueness."

And you can recover, too.

## Suggestions

*Do* realize things are just objects and will not make you feel better about yourself. Only by reaching within, to your core, will you begin to help yourself to feel stronger.

*Do* read self-help and inspirational books, become involved in community work, improve your mind—work toward reconnecting to your healthy self-esteem.

# CHAPTER ELEVEN

## *Staying Attached*

*No matter what the reality, home is where your heart is.*

"I am the second wife of a divorced man," says Lisa. "His divorce was final over seven years ago. His ex-wife, though, sees that they still have a relationship . . . she refers to it as THE DIVORCE. She lives to hate him. She is putting her health and her life energy on the sacrificial altar of 'divorce.' The one that suffers most is the child between them.

"A life unexamined is not worth living, as far as I'm concerned. And yet, a thousand dollars per month is our contribution to hers," says Lisa.

Before we fall into the misconception that only women have problems letting go, this is Dean's story, twice. His first marriage lasted for eight years. He has a daughter, Diana, who is now ten years old. She was born after four years of marriage. Dean and his wife had wanted to have a child, but the marriage started going downhill after his daughter's birth.

"Before Diana was born, my wife, Yvonne, was a self-sufficient, intelligent, career woman. After, she became 'the house mom,' which would have been fine if she had just taken a year off from work to be at home, but she never quite snapped out of it. I spent the next three years begging, pleading, and rationalizing with her—finally telling her point-blank that I wanted my wife back. There was no wife for me, only a super mom. For three years, I came home from work to find her wearing who knows what, her hair a mess, crawling around on the floor talking baby talk with our daughter. I wanted to come home to a woman. Then she started putting on weight."

Dean was a regional sales manager for a very large company and accepted a transfer to Boulder, Colorado, where they bought a beautiful home with a view. "Even that didn't help. It finally got down to my saying, 'Look Yvonne, I want YOU back, I want our marriage back, and I want a partner.' It was a very sad situation, and I was feeling very lonely. My only function, I felt, was to supply a paycheck. Yet, even though she turned into our daughter's playmate, I still had to do the discipline—she certainly didn't have a clue about real parenting."

Dean didn't want to end the marriage, he loved his wife and had always envisioned that they would be married forever. "But I couldn't deal with it any longer. Here she was, putting on weight while I watched her sit on the floor eating pizza. One night, while I was working out in the next room, I said to her, 'Why don't you join me? We'll spend some time together, and you can get into shape.' She yelled back, 'I don't care if I put on weight, I know you're having an affair.' I assured her that I wasn't but would if things didn't change.

"Nothing changed. I didn't have the affair, but a few months later I remember thinking—I'm thirty-three, I've been married eight years, do I want to do another eight years of this? A voice came up inside me and just screamed, 'NO!' For three years, I'd given her time to adjust. She didn't have to pursue a top-notch career again, like she had when I met her, but something. Yvonne loved material things, i.e. the bigger house, the better car. I always made good money, I'm not wealthy, but I thought we had a good life with nice things. If Yvonne wanted above-and-beyond fringes, she would have to pitch in. I thought that was fair. She had no job whatsoever, and by now our child was three years old."

There was no emotional intimacy left; he felt used. "When I tried to connect, it was ignored or rejected, our sex life went down to almost zero. I felt like an object, an American Express Gold Card. I asked her to go into therapy with me, but she didn't feel any need for it. Her life was just as she wanted it to be. Apparently there was a part of her that just always wanted to be kept by a successful husband, which would have been fine were she available to me emotionally. It finally came to a head over a new car she wanted to buy. Yvonne said she wanted another car. I told her to look for a used car, narrow her choices to a couple, and we'd go see them together. I came home from work one day to find out her choice was a new BMW Seven Series. I couldn't believe the nerve."

To Dean, the situation became clear. She didn't want to sleep with him, but she did want a BMW. He told Yvonne they couldn't afford the maintenance and insurance on the car, and if she wanted it, she would have to pitch in. "She just laughed and walked away from me. I told her I couldn't live like this anymore and was leaving. She turned around and said, 'You can't leave.' I'll never forget the look on her face or the way she said it, like it was an order that I couldn't disobey. I said, 'Watch me!' as I went to the closet and started grabbing my clothes. I threw them into my car and drove off. I left everything else.

"I was shattered—not living with Diana—and knowing I was responsible for breaking up our daughter's home. I blamed myself for that. And, of course, Yvonne used that as leverage. Because of the tremendous guilt I was feeling, I gave Yvonne our home, fully furnished, and took nothing. Several months later, the mortgage company called me at work to tell me that the house was in repossession, foreclosure, and what was I going to do about it? I told them it was no longer my house, that I'd given it to my wife in the divorce. Apparently she hadn't refinanced it so my name was still on the loan. They were coming after me!"

Dean telephoned her to find out that she had rented it out, was collecting the rent, but wasn't paying the mortgage company. "She wasn't even living there anymore, after all the guilt I had been feeling over breaking up my daughter's home. That really hurt. In business situations, I'm very shrewd, but when it comes to somebody I love and spent part of my life with, I don't look to get stabbed like that. I took a real bath on that.

"Yvonne also continues to try to turn my daughter against me with ludicrous lies. Even though I told her that she's only hurting our daughter, it hasn't stopped. When I moved out, she told her that I had left them *both*. The most off-the-wall stunt she pulled was to tell Diana I had put out a contract on Yvonne. One day, Diana called my mother and said, 'Grandma, mommy told me that daddy put out a contract on her.' My mother said, 'WHAT?' Not thinking a six year old really knows the meaning, my mother asked, 'What do you mean by a contract?' and Diana explained what a contract for murder is. Remember, the child is six years old. Now, of course, there was no truth to this. Not only was it a lie, but I'd never made idle threats or even joked along those lines. It was totally unfounded.

"Despite the heartaches, I felt good about leaving Yvonne because she was just using me. Regardless, my self-esteem dipped dramatically. Where did I go wrong? What did I do? How did this happen? I felt used and confused, not understanding how it had happened. But before I could begin to learn how to take care of myself, instead of taking care of a marriage that wasn't, I had to go through one more hurdle—my next marriage. It's unfortunate but true, wisdom only came to me through pain."

Dean quickly became involved in a relationship with a woman who had been a friend and associate at work. "She could see that I was upset. We went to lunch a few times. Within a couple of months, I was seeing her. Ten days after my divorce was final I was saying, 'I do.' Everyone warned me that I was simply on the rebound. No way. I'd been around the block a couple of times, was a big boy. I know it just *looked* that way.

"I rushed into this marriage, and it was different, it was filled with passion, and I was very much in love with Lisa. This marriage lasted three and a half years. We couldn't live together, it was a bad mistake for a myriad of reasons. I realize now that we were both working out childhood issues. But it was the most intense love experience and the most wonderful sex that I'd ever had. And the companionship. I was starved for a companion to explore my inner feelings and dreams with, a relationship that wasn't attached to some kind of monetary reward.

"When I divorced Lisa, it was the most horrible experience of my life. In a three-and-a-half-year marriage, we split up three times. The last time, it was devastating. I couldn't breathe, I felt like there was a hole in the center of my body. I walked around feeling like my guts were hanging out, literally. For the first time in my life, I got hives. I woke up one morning looking like a lobster. I was longing and yearning for this woman and, I thought, would never be able to re-place the part of me that she had filled. She felt the same way, that's why we kept getting together. For example, I left in 1990 and moved to another state. After six months of not even speaking to her, we had a phone conversation, she ended up coming out to visit me, and ninety days later I moved back into the house in Denver. We spent another year together."

Dean's second marriage, for far different reasons, was even more difficult to let go of than the first. In the first marriage, it was because of the child. In the second marriage, it was because of the marriage itself. "We tried everything to make it work. In retrospect, I knew it was never going to work because it was founded in very unhealthy things. Our relationship was the horrible part of letting go. With Yvonne, letting go of her was not the problem, the problem was de-stroying a family."

## Suggestions

*Don't* be surprised to discover that your heart and head are of two different minds.

*Do* what you must to set your life in order without involving the innocent, your children. Hold on to your sense of fair play, honor, and honesty.

# CHAPTER TWELVE

## *Feeling Guilty and Kids*
*You probably should. It's okay.*

Is a good divorce better, from a child's point of view, than a bad marriage? A new study may surprise you.

The Exeter study, which examined the impact of family breakup from the children's point of view, clearly demonstrates that children of divorced parents are more likely to be unhappy, unhealthy, and experience problems at school and with friends than are children of parents who quarrel but remain married.

Dr. John Tripp and Monica Cockett, of the department of child health at Exeter [England] University's medical school, interviewed 152 children ages nine to ten and thirteen to fourteen. Half came from intact families, both harmonious and quarrelsome, some violent; the other half came from divorced families. Among the latter, thirty-one lived with a single parent, twenty-six had become part of stepfamilies, and nineteen had been through three or more family reorganizations.

The children from intact and divorced families were matched by pairs according to six variables, including age, sex, and family background. The study is unusual in that the researchers focused on the children rather than their parents, asking about their family life, self-image, school, support needs, then followed up with parents, family doctors, and schoolteachers.

The children whose parents had parted were at least twice as likely as those from intact families to report low self-esteem, diffi-culties with friendships and schoolwork, and behavioral and health problems, especially psychosomatic disorders including stom-achaches, feeling sick, and bedwetting. The children's perceptions were confirmed by their parents.

The children of parents who were fighting but remained together experienced similar health and social problems, but the level and number of problems were closer to those of harmonious families than to those of divorced.

Feeling guilty yet? Problems for children of divorce are a reality which can't be ignored. Be sensitive to the needs of your children, whose struggles are as, if not more, serious than your own. Be aware that you and your children won't necessarily adjust at the same rate. Some children do so before their parents, sometimes the reverse: A child may continue to suffer, even though you have come to terms with the divorce and are building new lives. Then, too, children within a family may respond differently, one child gaining maturity and independence, another regressing. What can you expect?

You can expect that all children, almost without exception, are af-fected by divorce. How much, and for how long, depends on many factors, including age, sex, prior emotional resiliency, and perhaps most importantly, the availability of adult support. Even in families where parents have openly battled for years, children usually fear and resent a divorce. An older, more sophisticated child of feuding parents may recognize that a divorce is desirable but, nevertheless, feel worried and resentful.

Typically, the first year or two after separation is the most difficult time for all; by the end of the second year, most families find a bal-ance and have ironed out major difficulties. With time and *reduced parental conflict,* many children come to see the divorce more posi-tively. If the divorce separates a child from a seriously disturbed or violent parent, it often brings relief and new emotional gains.

Among children who cope successfully, the most important factors are love, interest, and caring from both parents on a day-to-day basis. A supportive, mature custodial parent sets the stage for a child's adjustment and well-being.

By nurturing your relationship with your child, and by encouraging a good relationship with your ex-spouse—regardless of problems—you offer the best protection to your children, and your children's children, for their mental health and future development.

Depending on the ages of your children, their responses will vary. Toddlers two to four often regress to a more dependent level, such as demanding to be fed instead of feeding themselves and reverting to diapers. In this age group, when sexual interest runs high and a parent of the opposite sex leaves, it is thought by some to be detrimental to the child's sexual development. At the same time, children this age often wish parents of the same sex out of the competition. When the parent actually leaves, the child is convinced he or she has caused it.

Children ages six to eight also assume responsibility for the split-up but fears of abandonment and starvation are often added to the mix. They are old enough to realize what's going on, but they don't have adequate skills to deal with it. Many experts agree this is the most critical age for children of divorce—and it is the one with the largest number of children affected.

Some children react by trying to gain control over what they feel to be chaos. Others, especially boys whose fathers have left, try to become the missing parent, assuming responsibilities that are not appropriate for their young age. In one study of twenty-six children of divorce between the ages of five and a half and seven, a pervasive sense of sadness was noted. Unlike toddlers who could fantasize that their families were still intact, these slightly older children could not, and they tended to dream up fanciful reasons for the divorce. "They only knew each other two days before getting married, and they should have known each other at least nine," one seven year old explained.

Between the ages of eight to twelve, children's most distinguishing emotion is anger directed at the parent thought to have initiated the divorce. The anger can erupt in classrooms and alienate friends just when they are most needed. At the same time, children at this age often form a very close relationship with one friend or with a teacher or another adult. Some transfer emotions from the noncustodial parent, which might set up a delayed reaction. For instance, a girl may choose father figures in people she later dates, looking for someone to take care of her.

Teenagers have a different set of problems. Unlike younger children, they feel little sense of blame for the separation of their parents, but they are saddled with the dilemma of loyalty when parents, even indirectly, force children to choose sides.

A child's gender also plays a part in the impact of divorce. Boys are the harder hit because more is expected of them while they might, unfortunately, receive far less support from their mothers, teachers, and peers. A boy might begin a destructive circle of bullying other children, then crying when they hit back, thus alienating boys his own age. A little girl, on the other hand, vents her sadness by crying—literally—for attention.

Cutting through all age and gender distinctions is an obsessive desire to reunite the parents.

In general, "A child living with his/her divorced mother, compared to a child living with both parents, is 375 percent more likely to need professional treatment for emotional or behavioral problems and is almost twice as likely to repeat a grade of school, is more likely to suffer chronic asthma, frequent headaches, and/or bedwetting, develop a stammer or speech defect, suffer from anxiety or depression, and be diagnosed as hyperactive," according to the National Center for Health Statistics.

About fifteen or twenty years ago, people were less aware, and a child was ostracized for not having a daddy living at home, but now it's pretty common. That does not, however, make it any easier emotionally for the child. Your goal as parents is to keep the wholeness of the child intact without the wholeness of the family for support.

## Suggestions

*Don't* be surprised to learn that most children would prefer their family stay intact despite problems, except abuse.

*Do* realize that children of divorce have special needs which you'll need to be sensitive to if they are to eventually see the divorce as positive.

*Do* encourage your children to maintain a good relationship with both parents. You're getting the divorce, not your children.

*Don't* encourage your child to become the parent.

# CHAPTER THIRTEEN

## *Kids as Property*
### *Kids as bargaining chips.*

Rebecca thought her separation and pending divorce were moving along pretty smoothly. Attorneys had been hired, and she congratulated herself on how well she and her soon-to-be ex-husband had worked out visitation details regarding the children. While living with her, they would spend every other weekend at their father's and at least one weekday evening with him.

Aside from his habitually picking up the children late, all was going well. Until a phone call came from her attorney. He had received a letter from her husband's attorney stating that unless Rebecca stopped fighting over a particular financial detail, her husband would no longer visit the children. She was astonished.

Rebecca recalls, "I couldn't believe my ears! I picked up the telephone and called my husband, asking if he had agreed to his attorney's threat. He knew nothing about it and, thank goodness, had no intention of ignoring the children, no matter what else was going on!

"At this point, I knew for certain things were way out of control. I convinced my husband to put the divorce attorneys on hold, and we went to see an arbitrator/therapist. Within three sessions, we had worked out the details the two attorneys found so insurmountable. We telephoned the attorneys with our agreement, and their legal work was quickly completed. I guess that's called 'taking control.' We saved a small fortune by not allowing our attorneys to fight back and forth between themselves. By using our children as pawns, the whole situation could go nowhere but downhill, especially for the kids."

When decisions affect your children, the two of you must take control of yourselves but not of each other through your children. You won't always find it easy to come to terms, but do your best—even before telling your children about the upcoming separation. Regardless of conflicts, resolve the issues of custody, visitation, finances, and continuing family relationships and friendships. If discussions end in nothing but an argument, get help—a counselor or member of the clergy may be needed to help resolve these questions.

"A standard behavior," says Los Angeles judge Richard E. Denner, "is for one parent to deny visitation to the other because they won't pay support. While, on the other hand, he refuses to pay support because she won't give him visitation."

Children aren't property. They're people with feelings, fears, and needs who haven't a clue how to deal with them—yet. You can help. Even very young children need to be prepared for separation and divorce. They need practical information, such as where they will live, who will take care of them, where they will go to school, and whatever other issues are of major concern to them. Young children fear that they will be left by both parents, that they will not have a roof over their heads, food to eat, or enough money for other needs.

Older children worry about moving away from friends or school and about lacking funds for college. Children also worry about where the noncustodial parent will live and the mechanics of how, and how often, they'll see them.

A better understanding of the way divorce affects children may help you to help your children put their lives back together again.

The effects of divorce on children became an urgent social question in the late 1970s and early 1980s, when the U.S. divorce rate reached an all-time peak. Although the rate has since begun to decline, divorce still affects a million or more children under age eighteen every year. In fact, twice as many children per 1,000 are affected by divorce today than were affected a generation ago.

Until recently, the assumption was that the divorce itself caused a child's negative behavior. Researchers, tracing the experiences of children before, during, and after divorce, have shown that many problems existed before the family breakup. The divorce was merely the *last* in a chain of events. When there is a history of family problems, divorce may be a marker—but not always the cause—for your children's problems. In the United States, a family usually breaks up over time—a period of years, not months.

Although divorce crosses all social and economic boundaries, even if the absent parent is scrupulous about paying child support, there may still be a drop in resources for the custodial parent, i.e. downward mobility. The costs of litigation and maintaining two households can reduce the family's income enormously. A lower standard of living, welfare dependency, a move to a poorer neighborhood, and other changes are stressful to everyone.

During that extended time of snowballing dysfunction, some children act out their pain with increasingly destructive behaviors, including substance abuse. The breakup itself provokes some children into exaggerating these behaviors. (The behavior of 35 percent of children worsens during divorce, nearly half exhibit no change, and nearly one in five shows improved behavior.)

Research shows that most children who exhibit these exaggerated behaviors do so for a relatively short time, not much longer than the classic two-year, postdivorce crisis time. After that, children usually return to their "normal" selves. Some, however, will have profound problems for many years after the actual breakup.

How long these problems continue depends, to a great extent, on how much conflict continues between you and your ex-spouse, on their access to both parents, on their changed economic circumstances, and on their established patterns of achievement and stability.

Many new questions are now being addressed with respect to both the short-term and long-term effects of divorce upon children.

The new data prompts researchers to see the breakup as one event within a series of events that are the history of a troubled family.

Many children trying to cope with the tension and stress of their parents' marriage, can be helped to weather the stress of divorce, and the damage afterward, with a preventive approach to child care.

With a million American children experiencing divorce each year, even a minority with long-term problems represents a significant number who need help overcoming the lingering effects, not only of divorce, but of the dysfunction that set the stage for the breakup of the family.

Getting back to the property issue in general, it's interesting to note that the assets which are the toughest to divide, according to Judge Denner, are the ones that cost the least, such as the family album. "We have a multitude of ways of handling this, but usually a copy is made of all the pictures and the cost of copying divided in half. Hopefully one side hasn't yet clipped the other side out of the pictures. The average person forgets some things that have to be divided, like the life insurance and pension plan, because they seem so far into the future that it's hard to even think about them.

"The hardest cases to deal with are those in which the husband has been totally involved in the daily economics and the wife wasn't. Sometimes, when I'm discussing court fees, support, etc., I feel like I'm speaking a foreign language. To some extent, both people are responsible for that situation because that was the choice they made. Those are often very hard cases to settle because the wife may be thinking—he was the one having the affair, so why should my life be upset? I've seen this happen time and time again. The husband has an affair so the wife initiates a divorce to 'bring him to his senses.' It backfires because he thinks it's a great idea."

## Suggestions

*Don't* use your children as pawns.
*Do* take control of yourself, not of each other through the divorce.

*Do* realize that your children's world has been turned upside down, and they also have fears.

*Do* be aware that there is a normal two-year adjustment period for you and your children, during which everyone may act out, needing patience and understanding.

# CHAPTER FOURTEEN

## *When to Tell the Kids*
*Think they don't know something's going on? They're scared and confused, too.*
*-and-*

## *What to Tell the Kids*
*A three year old's not a fifteen year old.*
*-and-*

## *How to Tell the Kids*
*Together*
*-and-*

## *Kids and Dating*
*Understanding and reassurance.*

If you tell the children too far ahead of the separation, they may think it's not going to happen or try to prevent it. If you wait until your spouse is walking out the door, you have waited too long. Children should have enough time to absorb the idea and to question both parents. How much time varies with their age and maturity.

Telling children once is usually not enough. In the days or weeks between the first discussion and the separation, an open dialogue should be established so that all of their questions can be answered and reanswered, important information repeated, and the children reassured. Repeated conversations can help you, your spouse, and the children to accept the reality of the situation. It can also help to establish the lines of communication and support so needed after separation.

What exactly do you tell your children? After all, a three year old's not a fifteen year old. What do children need to know? They need an understandable, age-appropriate explanation of the impending separation. Children don't need to know all the reasons that led to the divorce decision, although children may be more aware of them than you realize. For example, if an extramarital relationship is a factor in the divorce and children raise the issue, there should be no denial or blame. Older children can understand that the other person may be just symptomatic of the unhappiness that contributed to the failing marriage.

Children need to know the decision has not been made suddenly or frivolously. But what may seem rational to you may not seem so to children, particularly very young children.

One mother described her efforts to convince her two preschoolers she still loved them even though she felt compelled to leave. "I visit them often and reassure them of my love, but they are too young to understand that the situation at home was causing me to be seriously depressed. I hope someday when they are older, and if I keep a close relationship with them, they will understand and forgive me."

Children need to know they're free to love both of you, to express sadness, anger, and disappointment—but not to manipulate you by playing one against the other or to indulge in uncontrolled anger or destructive behavior. They need to know that discipline will be enforced by both parents, that they will be expected to obey agreed-upon ground rules—such as bedtime and chores—and that limits on behavior essential to their sense of well-being and security will be imposed.

Should children have a voice in the decision? If they are old enough, talking to you may help them feel they are part of the decision-making process and open lines of communication. Even older children should not have to choose between parents. Although most states allow older children to decide which parent to live with, few children want that responsibility, particularly right at the time of the divorce or separation.

Children's reactions vary according to their age, but almost without exception, they have difficulty accepting the separation at first. Children do not readily give up on their parents' marriage. They may harbor their reconciliation dreams for years, even when they know the marriage was not a happy one.

In time, most children learn to accept the inevitable. Some even come to believe it's for the best. Nevertheless, knowing that children of all ages can be seriously upset for months or years will better prepare you to cope and to help your children through this adjustment time.

Divorce researchers have found that young boys generally take longer than young girls to regain their emotional balance. But there are some indications that girls may have delayed reactions, tending toward more difficulties during adolescence and early adulthood. Studies show few long-term effects of divorce on children, but young women from broken homes were found to have somewhat more negative attitudes toward marriage than did their peers from intact marriages.

Preschoolers have difficulty understanding the concept of divorce. Having lost one parent from the home, often they fear losing the other. Bedtime, or temporary separations, may bring tears and tantrums, requiring special reassurance.

School-age children, better able to grasp the meaning of divorce, have more coping resources. They live in a wider world, with friends and teachers to turn to. Nevertheless, they, too, experience guilt and fear. One eight year old described it this way, "I was sure my parents broke up because of me. I didn't *know* why I felt that way, but that's the way I felt."

Profound grief and anger are typical reactions to the losses in your children's lives. And so, a child is particularly prone to building a long-term alliance with one parent against another. Developmental and school progress may have to take a temporary backseat, as children work out an emotional balance.

Adolescents react in many ways. As neither children nor adults, they swing back and forth between two worlds. Involvement in activities outside the home can provide distance from parental problems. A mature perspective can enhance understanding and reduce stress. On the other hand, teenagers are more often called upon by beleaguered parents for help. Some rise to the occasion and enjoy increased self-esteem; others find themselves overburdened, resentful, and confused.

Some adolescents turn to attention-seeking behaviors such as running away, stealing, or sexual promiscuity. Sexuality can be a major issue for both adolescents and parents. A youngster's concerns about sexual competency and marriage may be heightened by the divorce; the newly dating parent may be seen as a competitor. Parents worry about dating again, about their youngsters' acceptance of it, as well as providing good adult models for their opposite-sex youngsters.

This information should prepare you for some rough times, not lead you to believe that all is lost. Most children display amazing strengths.

Many children become supportive of the custodial parent, recognizing their new responsibilities and problems. Children often prove exquisitely sensitive to parents' needs and moods. Some develop closer relationships with both parents following separation.

A vital factor in children's adjustment is their relationship with the custodial parent, which is usually the mother. After an initial period of shock, most mothers are able to cope just fine with their added responsibilities. Children who can maintain close contact with their fathers as well generally have an emotional advantage.

A young women, recounting her experiences when her parents divorced reports, "The greatest gift my mother gave me was my relationship with my father. She never tried to turn me against him, and she encouraged our visits. It made things more comfortable for dad and me, and I will always love her for it."

Anything that provides stability to children—continued contact with grandparents and other family members, the same residence, school, church, and friends—helps in their adjustment.

How do you tell a child that his family is going to change? Together. How do you explain what you may not understand yourself? There's no easy way to prepare children, yet you must. It is also important that this discussion not be delayed until the divorce is at hand, because the physical leaving by one parent is so traumatic for children.

How you prepare your child will depend on your feelings and those of the other parent, the circumstances of the divorce, and the age of the child. The best scenario is for both parents to tell them together. But each situation is different; no two divorces are alike because no two families are alike. As a rule, however, children should be told of the impending separation in an honest, straightforward way—no lies, no excuses, and absolutely no false promises. Children not only sense and appreciate your honesty, but it will help them feel protected. If you don't know some of the answers to their questions, admit it. What you keep hidden or don't say will be just as important as what you do say. The more children know about what is happening, the more readily they may adapt to the situation. The unknowns often scare children more than the knowns.

Try to explain the changes that are about to take place, one building block at a time. "Here's how it's going to be," you might start. "Things will be different, but together we'll be able to handle it." Then, fill in the details, but don't overwhelm them with too much information. For example, if one of you expects to remarry soon after the divorce, it might be better to postpone this news until the children have adjusted to the separation.

Prepare yourself. There will be questions. Picture the world through your child's eyes, and you may be able to anticipate some of them: Why the separation? What is a divorce? When is it going to happen? Why? Who will take care of me? Where will I live? Will I have to choose between parents? Where will I go to school? The more questions, the more grateful you should be. When children are consistently unquestioning, they may not be coping well. Whether they ask or not, you can be sure that questions are on their minds. Your children also need answers in a way that does not blame *anyone*. Separate your personal problems from family issues.

"When my ex-husband and I talked to our children, ages five and seven," says Rebecca, "our older child asked all the questions. Questions like: Where will dad live, when will I see him, etc. She was understandably upset and showed her hurt and confusion with tears. I realized that my younger child, while taking it all in, was not asking questions or showing any emotion. I took him on my lap, hugged him, and said, 'I know that right now you have a huge tummyache. I also know that your tummy won't always hurt and that you will feel better soon.' Finally the tears flowed and question after question tumbled out of his mouth."

If possible, both parents together should tell the children about the divorce for several reasons. Even if only one parent does the explaining, it is easier for children to accept the situation if the other is present. When parents explain separately, a child is more apt to feel he must choose sides. And, if the parents' stories don't match, the child may be confused, not knowing who to believe, what to believe, or how to act toward either parent. If your spouse has already left, you will have to handle the telling alone; delay only makes it more difficult.

It may be best to tell all the children at the same time. The presence of siblings may cushion the shock and provide an important sense of support and family continuity.

Unlike the needs of your children, your need for adult companionship may bring you to cross ends. How do you handle their needs and yours, i.e., kids and dating? With understanding and reassurance.

"It's no wonder during this time that children would hate any man or woman you show an interest in, whether the child is still young or an adolescent," says family therapist, Patricia N. Allee, M.A.

"At the very least, a dating parent may become emotionally unavailable and, at worse, children might find a disturbing flock of new men or women flying in and out of their home. I see adults this happened to years ago, when they were teenagers, and the memory is still disturbing. If divorce occurs when children are teenagers, they often become very, very resentful of the men that come in. A resentment that can last into adulthood.

"It's frightening to them because they see themselves losing not only the parent who left the house—probably the father—but, their mother as well. Just because divorce is more acceptable today, it is no less traumatic to children. Children must experience and grieve their loss, just like you, before they can heal. You are their role model."

Be a good one. Don't let them think it's possible, or even advantageous to try to avoid normal feelings of grief by keeping yourself on a social whirlwind. Your entire family needs to feel their sadness in order to recover and grow. Avoiding the present won't make it go away—anymore than ignoring the past can erase it.

Out of control adult grieving, the complete opposite of emotional denial, is equally upsetting for children because they get the message that it's their job to take care of you. It's not. Instead, it's vital that you develop your own support system, sympathetic listeners who are there to *hear* you, not do the impossible, i.e., to fix you or your situation.

## Suggestions

*Do* tell the children together, with love and caring, without blame, aware of their feelings and knowing they see themselves as half of each of you.

*Do* explain the changes that will be happening in their lives in an age-appropriate way.

*Do* encourage questions and feelings to be aired.

*Don't* begin dating too soon or view it lightly. Keep your child's perspective in mind.

# CHAPTER FIFTEEN

## *When Marriage Ends and Divorce Begins*
*Closure, focus, new beginnings.*

Your focus has taken an important shift—the road has forked, and you redirect your energies from the marriage to separation and divorce. Your children's feelings may become more conflicted as resolution takes upsetting twists and turns.

During this time, children often turn to other adults for comfort and attention. Good. Encourage these supportive relationships. They can be important sources of stability to them and can offer you some needed relief.

Teachers and after-school programs, such as Banana Splits, can be an important resource for school-age children. But, while school can offer escape from the stress at home, it can also be the stage for behavioral problems and failures. Let your child's teacher know what's going on at home. Informed teachers are better equipped to understand a child's problems and extend a helping hand.

In the following, ten to fourteen-year-old children tell their own stories, in their own words, of how it felt when their parents divorced or just fought about it. How could these situations have been less traumatic?

\*     \*     \*

### David

"When my parents first split up, it affected me a lot. A got real fat and my grades went down, so I went to a psychologist. She made me do a lot of things I thought were dumb, like draw pictures and answer lots of silly questions. My grades went down because I couldn't listen very well, I was always thinking about what was happening at home. It's not something I talk about very much though. Most of my friends would rather talk about MTV than talk about divorce."

### Laura

"My mom and dad got divorced three years ago. I did not feel bad at all. I didn't really notice at all. A few years later, my dad got together with Gail and married her. Then Gail got pregnant. I got a puppy. And my puppy likes my cat. Soon I will have a stepbrother or sister."

### Cathy

"My mom and my dad were talking about divorce. My mom told my sister and I that they were going to get a divorce. I started crying, and she yelled to my dad to talk to us. I was afraid that I would not be able to see my father again. He told us that he would come to see us and that he would take us to Disneyland, but I said that I didn't want to go anywhere, I just wanted them to stay together. After they talked to us, we went to see the TV.

"Later, when we were eating dinner, my dad told us that he wanted to talk to us again. They were not going to get a divorce. We were so happy when he told us that."

### Kevin

"My mom and dad got divorced. Now I have two moms and two dads. One dad is my stepdad and one mom is my stepmom. I didn't want my parents to get a divorce, but they did. I was so unhappy and I cried so much—I wish they were still together. My life changed a lot. I had to go to a different school and live in a new house. I could not see my mom for a long time."

**Thomas**

"I live with my dad, and my sister lives with my mom. I like that because we can switch around when we want. My friend, Sam, says that his parents fought over him, and he felt like a check in a restaurant—you know, the way it is when two people grab for the check and one says, 'I'll pay it,' and the other one says, 'No, this one is mine.' Secretly neither one really wants it, they just go on pretending until someone finally grabs it, and then that one is stuck."

**Shawn**

"My dad got married to my stepmom. After the marriage, I became a big stepsister. Now I tell my friends all about them. I feel happy because I love my stepmom. I also love my stepbrothers. I'm also happy because my dad is happy. My life changed because I am no longer the only child. I became the oldest child. But, my stepbrothers drive me crazy!"

**Devyn**

"My mom and dad separated because my mom would drink in front of my little sister sometimes. When we'd come home from school, my mom would be drunk. Later my mom would start to get mad, and my parents would fight. This made me feel bad because we would always have to take her to my grandma's house. Then we'd have to sleep at my other grandma's house. Or sometimes my mom would stay at the house and, the next day, would be better. My dad could not take it, so my mom moved to a place where they were able to help her. Then she moved to her own house. Now we see her on the weekends."

**Pamela**

"My mom and dad are separated from each other. They separated in 1988, but I don't know why. It is a sad feeling. It also makes me feel mad. It changed my life because I don't see my dad anymore. But I feel good when he calls me, and he always sends me stuff."

**Sean**

"When my parents split up, we stayed with our cousin for about two months. I saw my father whenever he visited us. I was always happy to see him, but sometimes it made me feel sad, too, because I would look forward to our visits so much, and then when we were together, it could never be as perfect as I was hoping it would be. He was still so angry at mommy's leaving him that it was hard for him to feel good about anyone else.

"One good thing that happened was Big Brothers. They paired me off with a great guy, and we've been getting together every weekend. We play baseball or video games and eat hot dogs. His parents got divorced when he was twelve, and when I feel sad, I can talk to him."

### Gina

"When my mom and dad fight about getting a divorce, I get out of the house. It makes me feel sort of nervous. I want to leave my parents' house and live at my grandmother's. But if I left my family, I would get lonely."

### Richard

"When my parents were married, I hardly ever saw my dad because he was always busy at work. Now I've gotten to know him more because I'm with him every weekend. It's great. Like going to Disneyland because there's no set schedule, no 'Be home by five-thirty' kind of stuff. And my father is always buying me presents.

"The problem is that my mom got remarried and divorced again, so I've gone through two divorces so far. And my father's also gotten remarried—to someone I don't get along with all that well. It's made me feel that people shouldn't get married—they should just live together so they don't have to end up hating each other. The worst part is about money. Although my father buys me stuff, I feel bad because my mom says he owes her money. Sometimes I fight for my mom and sometimes for my dad, but I wish they'd leave me out of it completely. I feel caught in the middle."

### Roger

"My parents are divorced, and I have problems with them which I cannot resolve. My parents don't pay attention to me. In second and third grade, I had good grades. I tried hard to get those grades and to get their attention, but they didn't notice so I decided not to get good grades because it didn't help.

"So now I'm in fifth grade, and I still have that problem. I can't change because I think it is too late. That is the reason that I act bad at school. I know that this is not a good reason not to do my work. I spend all my time thinking about why I can't get their attention. I have a brother and sister and am the little one of the family."

### Brendon

"My parents were divorced when I was two, and I went to live with my mom. She couldn't take care of me so she was going to put me up for adoption. My dad didn't want that to happen, and so they had a big fight, and I went to live with my dad. One weekend, while I was visiting my mother, she and her boyfriend packed up their car with a lot of stuff, and we all piled in. When I asked her where we were going, she wouldn't tell me but said it would take two days to get there. I remember asking her about daddy, and she just told me not to worry about it.

"We went to another state, and she put me in school. Because she didn't want to send for my school records, she put me in kindergarten instead of where I belonged, in first grade. School was boring because it was so easy. I already knew the alphabet and dumb stuff like that. I wasn't there for very long because we moved one night. We climbed out the window of the apartment and drove off. Then I went to another school, which was better because I was at least in the right grade.

"One day the principal came into my classroom and told me to pack up my stuff, someone had come to pick me up. It was my father. I took my first plane ride, which was a lot of fun, and we went to my old home. That night we had a big party, all my father's family and friends came, and everyone was hugging me. I haven't seen my mother since then. I was so happy to be home, but I feel sad, too, because I miss my mother.

## Suggestions

*Do* be aware that your children's lives have been deeply affected by the changes in your lives, and their needs must be carefully addressed.

*Don't* assume they simply adapt without experiencing their own fears and grief just because they're children and that their fear and grief, if ignored, will not be lasting.

# PART TWO

## SEPARATION

"Being Divorced Is Like Being Hit By A Mack Truck. If You Live Through It, You Start Looking Very Carefully To The Right And To The Left."

*Jean Kerr, playwright,* Please Don't Eat The Daisies

# CHAPTER SIXTEEN

## *Lawyers: Yours, Mine, or Ours*
*Are you really saving money by using one attorney, or is one of you getting shortchanged?*

Among some Pueblo Indian tribes, a woman could divorce her husband simply by leaving his moccasins on the doorstep. Before you run at lightning speed for your husband's closet, remember the operative word here is "could." In today's legally complicated world, one pair of moccasins does not a divorce make.

One lawyer or two? "A lawyer really cannot serve two masters," says Judge Richard E. Denner, supervising judge for the Superior Court, Family Law Division, in Los Angeles. "If you've been to a mediator or have been able to come to an agreement yourselves and only need a lawyer to write it out and file the papers, that's one thing. Otherwise there's a danger. A single lawyer can't advise one party helpfully without hurting the other."

Of course, in today's imperfect world, not everyone has wonderful things to say about lawyers, specifically the lawyer that handled their divorce. Richard, working on his fourth marriage, says, "I was out of the country during my first divorce. And so, the judgment specified that I did not have to pay any child support. However, I also do not have visitation rights with my two children.

"My second divorce took place while I was a college student in

Honolulu. I had another child, but since I didn't have sufficient income to pay child support, once again, it was waived.

"My third divorce took place in Taiwan. I'd married a Chinese woman so that she and her two daughters could live in the United States. Having second thoughts, I told her I could not stay married just for her convenience. And so it went.

"I, personally, choose not to mess with lawyers. I let my ex's handle that. I do, however, have some pretty strong feelings about marriage and divorce. The person filing for the divorce should not be allowed to have anything from their spouse. A marriage is for better or worse, in sickness and in health, to death do you part. When a person wants to leave, they should leave everything, including the money your spouse worked so hard to earn."

Richard is feeling pretty victimized by both the courts and his ex-spouses, wouldn't you say? The legal process might be torturous, but that doesn't mean you should absolve responsibility for, or participation in, the process. Don't give up control just because it gets difficult—only to moan and groan about what you didn't get. Take it one step at a time. First step, the lawyer.

Once you have chosen a law firm to represent you, begin by putting together a list of the basics. What are the firm's office hours? Can after-hours or Saturday appointments be arranged if necessary? Learn the names of the staff—people who are on your team to help you—your attorney, the associate attorney, paralegal, secretary, bookkeeper, and receptionist. Keep this list by the phone. Note the name and address of the court at which your action is pending. Where is parking available?

Fees are explained during the initial interview. Ask questions about any part of the fee agreement you don't understand. Most law firms will begin work only after you have signed a fee agreement and paid an initial deposit (or retainer). After that, you'll receive monthly statements detailing their legal services and charges and the amount drawn from your deposit. If you have questions about your statement, call your lawyer's bookkeeper within ten days of receiving your bill.

Even though you may be seeking reimbursement of legal fees

from your spouse by court order, you are responsible for your attorney's fees. Any court order requiring your spouse to reimburse you is incidental to your responsibility to your lawyer.

If you need to contact your lawyer by phone, call during business hours. If he or she is in conference or court, a staff member will generally try to help you. Keep in mind that when you speak with your lawyer over the telephone, you will probably be billed for their time just as if you were sitting in their office.

Your lawyer's office is not the place for children and isn't an arena they should be involved in. Your divorce action is serious business and should be treated as such.

Keep important paperwork organized. This will help you feel some measure of control. *Read* all correspondence from your firm, and keep it together in a safe place. To keep you informed, your lawyer will provide you with copies of all pleadings and correspondence throughout the case.

Your lawyer needs ALL the facts. If you are nervous or afraid to tell your lawyer something, it may be easier to put it in writing. Whether you write or tell, you are your lawyer's eyes and ears—and, they must have all pertinent information. Your lawyer should know which information is critical to your case and which is not.

Don't hesitate to call the office if any questions or problems arise. Explain the matter to a staff member who should have an immediate solution or arrange to get back to you. If you find yourself calling constantly, try making a list of questions and save them for one call. This will help you to prioritize and focus your concerns and allow your lawyer to proceed with your case in an organized and coherent manner. Start keeping a daily diary, a record of events. Document which questions arise and when.

Write down in detail any problems or questions that worry you and forward them to your lawyer. This not only helps provide direct information and enables your lawyer to pinpoint and perhaps head off future problems, but this record becomes a part of your file for future use and review.

This is your life and your divorce. Stay informed, participate, and take responsibility for your decisions. There are variables, however, when it comes to the law and your divorce. At the beginning of a lawsuit, it may be difficult for your lawyer to know how long the case will take. After it is underway and your lawyer understands the issues, he or she should be better able to gauge the duration depending on:

- The number and complexity of contested issues, i.e. fighting between you and your spouse;
- The vehemence of your feelings and your inclination to settle;
- The court's calendar. A hearing can usually be scheduled within ten to fifteen days. A full divorce trial, which takes a day or more, usually must be scheduled six months to one year in advance;
- The other lawyer. Your lawyer has no control over the other lawyer's schedule or personality. An extremely busy or uncompromising opposing counsel can prolong your divorce.

But, by far, the most common factors that prolong lawsuits are the intensity of your feeling and the degree that you and your spouse are prepared to battle.

It is difficult to estimate realistically the total cost of your divorce, even when your lawyer knows the issues that will be contested and the strength of your feelings. If you and your spouse have little trust for each other and want complete "discovery" of all assets and liabilities, and issues are argued to the bitter end, the process will be long, drawn out, and *expensive*. Going to trial is almost always more expensive than settling the lawsuit.

You'll be paying for your divorce in three ways—with your time, emotions, and money. First, you will have to spend time preparing your lawsuit. Then, your lawyer will have to spend time, with your help, preparing your lawsuit. Lawyers sell their time, so if you can do some of the groundwork, do, so that your money can be used more efficiently. If you are not prepared to spend time on your case, you may not be as satisfied with the outcome nor will it be as cost-effective as it might have been.

Divorce is, without a doubt, one of life's most painful experiences. Your emotions will be on a roller coaster. In most divorces, one of you initiated the breakup, and so, one of you is hurting more emotionally. True? Consider counseling rather than using the courts as a battleground. Counseling can help you to deal with, and to accept, the end of your marriage. You'll also learn coping skills and how to pick up the pieces of your life and go on. Don't wait for your spouse to agree to counseling; individual counseling can help, with or without their participation. However, parents and children often attend sessions together.

The more issues to be resolved, the more traumatic the divorce process. One of you might even raise issues simply to prolong the process (in order to stay connected or to up the cost), to punish your spouse. Be aware. If this seems to be happening, it is hopeful your lawyer will call it to your attention.

In a divorce proceeding, feelings of hostility can delay a resolution and increase cost. Many factors may be involved in the breakup, and you may want to punish your spouse by making the process difficult and time consuming. This usually turns into a no-win situation. On the other hand, when perspective and a realistic idea of a fair settlement is maintained, less money will be spent on legal fees, leaving more for you, your spouse, and the support of children.

If you don't know where to begin, your lawyer will recommend qualified counselors. Your employment, social, or religious contacts might also provide leads. Check your local community services for counselors who can provide help on a sliding fee scale. When choosing a counselor, be selective. Counselors have different styles and approaches. Search until you find one with whom you feel comfortable. At the first meeting, ask about the cost. Find out if your health insurance policy will cover counseling. While reassurance from friends and family members and legal advice from your lawyer helps, a counselor is trained to address your emotional ups and downs.

One of the key factors in settling a divorce is your desire and ability to set aside differences and past hurts. Lawyers often hear, "It's a matter of principle. I won't compromise on this." A fair and equitable resolution may be reached, but you're at an impasse because of one inexpensive item. So you spend thousands of dollars in additional legal fees because of the lava lamp that nobody really wanted anyway. Only the lawyers come out ahead in a lengthy and bitter battle.

When you first go to a lawyer's office to discuss divorce, you may or may not be ready to take that big step. First you want to know your options. Perhaps you want advice on how to protect yourself and meet your needs, short of divorce. If your lawyer raises the issue of reconciliation, he or she is not questioning or judging your decision but is clarifying and confirming that you know your options and that you do want a divorce.

Preparing and trying a lawsuit is very expensive. Carefully consider all your issues early on. Which ones can and should be settled? You needn't make unreasonable or unnecessary concessions, but look carefully at the issues that separate you and your spouse. You do have some control, and you can make concessions that will resolve your case more quickly, saving you time and expense. Litigation often spawns more litigation. Decide the issues worth litigating, weigh the price you will pay with your time, emotions, and money.

Some people think that lawyers who are "fighters" must refuse to cooperate with opposing counsel—for example, not consenting to mutually convenient dates for meetings, depositions, etc., and refusing to compromise on contested issues. A sadly misguided notion. The time to fight is during tough negotiations or in court. The only thing noncooperation gets you is a larger bill because of all the legal steps that must be done the hard way—such as preparing special documents, appearing in court, etc. Information and documents must be disclosed eventually, and so, a lack of cooperation serves no purpose.

Lawyers who specialize in a particular area, such as family law, will probably try a number of cases against each other over the years. They will attend the same professional events and may even work on committees together. Camaraderie develops naturally over the years. Just because your lawyer and your spouse's lawyer exchange pleasantries, share a joke, or have lunch together, does not mean that they are being disloyal to you. Your lawyer is professionally committed to the best results for you given the facts of your case and the law. This does not mean that your lawyer must be hostile or mean to opposing counsel. Such behavior often harms rather than helps your case.

Try not to routinely reject your spouse's (or their lawyer's) suggestions just because you think they're either bad ideas or reflect an ulterior motive. Clients have been known to automatically do the opposite of whatever is requested. Let your lawyer help guide your response to their requests. A request, suggestion, or offer from the other side is not necessarily bad. Most lawyers are not out to "get, trick, or ruin" opposing counsel or their clients.

These, somewhat simplified, definitions will help you to understand what is happening with your divorce. The definitions may vary slightly from state to state.

*Action:* The legal term for lawsuit.

*Affidavit:* A written statement of facts made under oath and signed before a notary public.

*Affirmation:* A written statement of facts made and executed by a lawyer under penalty of perjury.

*Affirmative defense:* Legal response to a spouse's pleadings (even if the allegations of the petition for divorce are true).

*Agreement:* A written document stating what you and your spouse agree to.

*Alimony:* Payment of support from one party to another; may include property division and attorney's fees. *See also* maintenance.

*Alimony pendente lite:* A court order that provides temporary support for one spouse and/or the children while the divorce is in progress.

*Allegation:* Statement of what one spouse intends to prove.

*Annulment:* The legal ending of an invalid marriage; according to law, neither party was ever married, but all children born of the annulled marriage remain legitimate. Grounds for annulment vary from state to state.

*Answer:* The response of the spouse who didn't file for the divorce, separation, or annulment. It may admit or deny allegations and may also make claims against the other party.

*Appeal:* The process whereby a higher court reviews the proceedings or findings of a lower court and determines whether there was reversible error.

*Appearance:* A respondent's formal method of telling the court that he or she submits to the court's jurisdiction. Appearance can also refer to a party's physical presence at court.

*Change of venue:* A change in the location where the case is to be tried.

*Child support:* Support for a child (not taxable to the recipient or deductible to the payer spouse).

*Claim:* A charge by one spouse against the other.

*Common-law marriage:* A relationship between a man and a woman, recognized by law in some states as a marriage, although no license or ceremony was involved. The termination of a common-law marriage takes place by a divorce.

*Community property:* Generally, the property acquired during the marriage by the work and efforts of the parties. Applies in those states known as community-property states.

*Contempt of court:* The willful failure to comply with a court order, judgment, or decree which may be punishable in a variety of ways.

*Contested case:* Any case in which the court must decide one or more issues on which the parties have not agreed.

*Court order:* A written document issued by the court, which becomes effective when signed by a judge.

*Cross-examination:* The questioning of a witness by the opposing lawyer during a trial or at a deposition, to test the truth of that testimony or to develop it.

*Custody:* The legal right and responsibility awarded by the court for the care, possession, and rearing of a child.

*Default or default judgment:* A judgment by the court made without hearing the other side because it failed to submit papers on time or failed to appear at the hearing.

*Defendant (respondent):* The person (husband or wife) who is sued for divorce.

*Deposition:* The testimony of a witness taken outside of the court under oath and in writing.

*Direct examination:* The initial questioning of a witness by the lawyer who called him or her to the stand.

*Disclosure, discovery, or production of documents:* Procedures to determine the nature, scope, and credibility of the opposing party's claim and his or her financial status.

*Dissolution:* The act of terminating a marriage; divorce; does not include annulment.

*Distributive award:* A payment ordered by the court.

*Emancipation:* The point at which a child may be treated as an adult and in some states when the duty to support may terminate.

*Equitable distribution of property:* A system of distributing property based on a variety of factors without regard to who holds title.

*Evidence:* Documents, testimony, or other materials offered to the court to prove or disprove allegations.

*Ex parte:* An application for court relief without the presence of the other party.

*Grounds:* In the eyes of the law (under statute), the reason for granting a divorce.

*Guardian ad litem (GAL):* A person appointed by the court to represent the children.

*Hearing:* Any proceeding before the court for the purpose of resolving disputed issues through presentation of testimony, offers of proof, and arguments.

*Hold-harmless:* A situation in which one spouse assumes liability for a debt or obligation and promises to protect the other from any loss or expense in connection with it.

*Indemnification:* The promise to reimburse another person in case of an anticipated loss; the same as holding harmless.

*Injunction:* A court order forbidding someone from committing a particular act that is likely to cause injury or property loss to another party; the same as a restraining order.

*Interrogatories:* A series of written questions served on the opposing party to discover certain facts regarding disputed issues. The answers to interrogatories must be under oath and served within a prescribed period of time.

*Joint custody:* The shared right and responsibility awarded by the court to both parents for possession, care, and rearing of the children.

*Joint property:* Property held in the name of more than one person.

*Jurisdiction:* The authority of the court to rule on issues relating to the parties, their children, or their property.

*Legal separation:* A judgment of the court or written agreement directing or authorizing the spouses to live separate and apart. A decree of separation does not dissolve the marriage and does not allow the parties to remarry.

*Maintenance:* Spousal support. *See also* alimony.

*Marital property:* Accumulated income and property acquired by the spouses, subject to certain exclusions in some states.

*Marital settlement agreement:* The parties' settlement reduced to a written document or orally placed on the record in open court. May also be called a property settlement agreement.

*Motion:* A written application to the court for some particular relief such as temporary support, injunction, or attorney's or expert's fee.

*Motion to modify:* A formal written request to the court to change a prior order regarding custody, child support, alimony, or any other order that the court may change by law.

*Motion to vacate premises:* A request to the court, on the showing of good cause, ordering one spouse to leave the marital residence.

*No-fault divorce:* When divorce is granted without the necessity of proving one of the parties guilty of marital misconduct. Fault is marital misconduct that may be considered for some issues in some states.

*Notice of hearing:* A paper that is served on the opposing lawyer or other spouse listing the date and place of a hearing and the motions that will be heard by the court.

*Order:* The court's ruling on a motion regarding the parties to do certain things or setting forth their rights and responsibilities. An order is reduced to writing, signed by the judge, and filed with the court.

*Party:* The person in a divorce action whose rights and/or interests are to be affected by the divorce.

*Petition (complaint):* The first pleading in an action for divorce, separate maintenance, or annulment, setting forth the allegations on which the requested relief is based.

*Petitioner (plaintiff):* The party who files the petition for divorce or any other petition.

*Plaintiff:* The petitioner.

*Pleading:* Formal written application to the court for relief and the written response to it. Pleadings include petitions, answers, counterclaims, replies, and motions.

*Privilege:* The right of a spouse to make admissions to his or her spouse, or a lawyer, member of the clergy, psychiatrist, doctor, or certified social worker that are not later admissible in evidence.

*Pro se:* A litigant who is not represented by a lawyer (also *pro per*).

*Relief:* Whatever a party to a divorce proceeding asks the court to do: dissolve the marriage, award support, enforce a prior court order or decree, divide property, enjoin certain behavior, dismiss the complaint of the other party, and so on.

*Reply:* The pleading filed in answer to the allegations of a counterclaim.

*Report of referee with notice:* The written recommendations of a referee, or court-appointed officer, made after a hearing. It is not law or an order of the court but what is recommended to be an order of the court.

*Respondent (defendant):* The one who defends the divorce proceeding brought by another.

*Request for production of documents:* Documents and/or other information to be produced.

*Rules of evidence:* The rules that govern the presentation and admissibility of oral and documentary evidence at court hearings or depositions.

*Separate property:* Property that is not "marital property."

*Setoff:* A debt or financial obligation of one spouse that is deducted from the debt or financial obligation of the other spouse.

*Settlement:* Agreement on disputed issues.

*Show cause:* Written application to the court for some type of relief, which is made on the other party as the court directs.

*Stipulation:* An agreement between the parties or their counsel.

*Subpoena:* A document served on a party or witness requiring appearance in court. Failure to comply with the subpoena could result in punishment by the court. A subpoena *duces tecum* is a subpoena requesting documents.

*Summons:* A written notice that legal action has begun, requiring a response within a specified time period.

*Temporary or pendente lite motions:* Applications to the court for interim relief pending the final decree. Typical motions are for child support, attorney's fees, costs, expert fees, custody, visitation, enforcement or modification of prior temporary orders, or requests for exclusive possession.

*Temporary restraining order (TRO):* An order of the court that prohibits a party from doing something—for example, threatening, harassing, or beating the other spouse and/or the children, selling personal property, taking money out of accounts, denying him or her a motor vehicle.

*Testimony:* Statements under oath by a witness in court or during a deposition.

*Transcript:* A typewritten record of testimony taken by a court reporter during a deposition or in court.

*Trial:* A formal court hearing to decide disputed issues.

*Uncontested divorce:* A proceeding in which a person sued for divorce does not fight it or may have reached an agreement with the spouse during the divorce proceedings.

Lawsuits proceed in different ways. If you institute the suit, you will be referred to as "plaintiff" or "petitioner." Your spouse will be the "defendant" or "respondent." Your lawyers will file papers (a "petition" or "complaint") with the proper court and request service ("delivery") of the papers to the defendant. Generally the completed papers will be submitted to you for approval before they are filed. After the papers have been delivered to the defendant, the law provides a specific time during which he or she may respond to your petition. This period may be extended by the court or by agreement between the attorneys.

Dissolving a marriage requires that everyone work together so that a bad situation doesn't get worse. It is in both your best interests to act in a civilized, courteous manner and to negotiate in a way that will defuse tensions, avoid hostility, and maximize you (and the lawyers') ability to arrive at a fair and reasonable settlement.

Experienced family lawyers know, and countless studies confirm, that an agreement *negotiated* between you and your spouse is the best possible outcome, because it allows them to fine-tune matters that courts are ill-equipped to resolve. After all, the court will never know your case as well as you and your lawyers do.

Some cases, despite everyone's best efforts, cannot reach a settlement. This may be the result of unrealistic expectations, a dispute over the facts or the law, novel circumstances or issues, or your (or your spouse's) unwillingness to grant the other a divorce. No settlement can be reached without your consultation and approval.

Once the divorce is filed, it may be necessary to get some kind of immediate relief: such as a restraining order; immediate temporary support; control of assets; custody and visitation orders; a right to remain in the home; or, payment of attorney's fees. If so, your lawyer will file the motion, and the judge will sign an order directing your spouse to appear for a court hearing on why the court should not grant the relief. This hearing usually is within a few weeks after the papers are filed and served. These temporary orders, sometimes called "pendente lite," may be changed again during the divorce case or at judgment (when your case is settled or tried).

At temporary relief hearings, the court may take testimony or may proceed on the basis of the documents filed or the lawyers' offers of proof. Time generally is limited, and many courts prefer not to take testimony.

Support needs for children and/or one of the divorcing spouses are one of the most common reasons for an immediate hearing. At this hearing, if you are seeking support, for example, you will present evidence of your needs, obligations, expenses, and income. Your spouse will also present evidence of his or her expenses, debts, and income. In most states, temporary child and spousal support is based solely on your incomes and on state or local support guidelines. For this reason, it is important to prove your income and your spouse's income early in the process. Help your lawyer put together a complete financial history by providing all the documents you can find that have anything to do with income.

The temporary support set at this first hearing is important. Temporary orders are usually in effect from ninety days to the end of trial. You may also ask the court to rule on other issues, such as who should remain in the family home during the divorce proceeding, who will control certain assets (such as a car), and who is responsible for certain debts.

The next stage is usually a "discovery" period, during which you and your spouse collect information necessary for settlement discussions and/or trial. Discovery is accomplished through interrogatories, depositions, and requests for documents.

In a default or uncontested divorce, only one of you will go to court, and this appearance will be relatively brief. (A respondent defaults if he or she fails to answer within the allotted time. A divorce is uncontested if the parties reach a compromise on every issue.) Testimony may be needed to prove that grounds for divorce exist. The judge will then grant a "judgment of dissolution of marriage." The plaintiff will sign the judgment, prepared by his or her attorney. Some states do not require a court appearance in a default or uncontested case. The judgment and other documents are simply submitted to the court.

If it seems unlikely that your case will be settled, or if your lawyer thinks that having a trial date might encourage settlement, he or she will request a trial date. After all pretrial discovery has been completed, the case will be scheduled for trial.

In some areas of the country, pretrial conferences are mandatory and serve to bring attorneys and clients together before the judge for the purpose of settlement. The pretrial conference is not a trial; no witnesses need be alerted. If at a pretrial conference, you and your spouse are able to settle all matters in dispute, the resolution is usually recited on the record (before the judge and court reporter). If settlement is not reached, another pretrial conference or the trial may be scheduled. Without your agreement on all issues, the case is contested and a trial is necessary. However, preparing for trial is intense, time consuming, and expensive.

At the trial, witnesses may be called and records subpoenaed to substantiate your position and your spouse's position on support, custody, property, or other issues. Testimony may be introduced to show jurisdiction (that this is the appropriate court to rule on the matter) and the legal grounds for divorce. However, the balance of the testimony will focus on matters in dispute and will take a relatively short time.

The judge will render a decision immediately after hearing all the testimony or study it further and inform your lawyers by mail, within a few days or, occasionally, several weeks or months. After the judge notifies the lawyers of the decision, they may further clarify or argue points before the ruling becomes a formal judgment. The judge will ask one of the lawyers to prepare the judgment for dissolution of marriage for approval by the other lawyer. Then the judge will sign and enter the judgment.

The time between the filing of a response to a divorce petition and the trial date will depend on the court's backlog and the time the case is expected to take. Nine months to a year is not unusual.

In most states, a marriage cannot be dissolved until a specific time has elapsed after the respondent receives the summons and petition or files an appearance, whichever occurs first. Other matters vary by state, such as which court will hear the case, how long you must live in a state before filing for divorce, and the waiting period between commencement of an action and the judgment.

Perhaps you want to become single and thus eligible to remarry before all the issues in the divorce are resolved—property division, support, or custody. In some states, it is possible to bifurcate the divorce, which means divide it in two. The issue of marital status is separated from all other issues by stipulation or court order.

Documents contain a great deal of information that will help your attorney prepare for settlement or trial. Your attorney will indicate which items you will need. Here's a sample list: Financial affidavit; estimated taxes; income tax returns; personal-property tax returns; banking information; financial statements; loan applications; broker's statements; stocks, bonds, and mutual fund certificates; stock option records; pension, profit sharing, deferred compensation agreements, and retirement plans; wills and trust agreements; life insurance policy; general insurance policies; outstanding debts; accounts payable and receivable; cash receipts books; real property; sale and option agreements; personal property; motor vehicles; corporate interests; partnership and joint venture agreements; employment records; fringe benefits; employment contracts; business records; charge account statements; membership cards; judgments;

gifts; charitable contributions; medical bills; monthly telephone and long-distance charges business related; tapes and photographs; and a safe-deposit box inventory.

Divorce mediation is a process whereby you negotiate some or all of the terms of the divorce with the aid of a third, neutral person—a mediator. The fundamental idea is to avoid the adversarial, win-or-lose situation that all too often develops when a divorce is settled by attorneys for each of you.

The mediator's role is to open up a discussion, encourage each spouse to be honest and accurate in order to reduce anger and hostility. The mediator is an impartial guide, usually a mental health professional such as a social worker or psychologist. Mediation is a cooperative, psychologically oriented approach to help you focus on your major needs and objectives and compromise on less essential ones. It smooths the way for a stubborn partner, or one with unrealistic expectations, into moving forward with the negotiations.

A mediator charges, on average, about half to two-thirds what an attorney would charge. Once an agreement between you and your spouse has been agreed on, your attorneys will step in to complete the legal process.

## Suggestions

*Do* understand the legal ramifications of your divorce. Stay aware of all proceedings.

*Don't* be victimized by the legal system, your ex-spouse, or lawyer. Seek the most knowledgeable help you can find but remain in control.

# CHAPTER SEVENTEEN

## *Who Am I?*

*When half of a whole feels like zero.*

One day the two of you were a couple—the next day, you're not. Separating physically was a breeze compared to the emotional job ahead—a process that, in part, involves the recognition that you're a whole person *all by yourself*. Physically, the separation might been clean and simple, but emotionally you feel like you're living a life filled with land mines.

At the outset, it it usually the woman who seems destroyed, while the man, to all external appearances, sails on smoothly. After all, a man still has his job to tell him who he is. His identity has always included the roles of husband and possibly father, but its largest component has been the image of independent, self-sufficient wages earner. Often he also has hobbies which reinforce his strong-man facade. A woman, on the other hand, especially if a homemaker, has put all her emotional eggs in one basket and when the bottom drops out, feels her identity has been completely shattered. But has it really?

"What you have to be willing to do," says Dee Shepherd-Look, Ph.D., professor of psychology at California State University at Northridge, "is to go back through the process of forming your identity, back to that adolescent experience of identity versus role confusion.

"In fact, if you married before your midtwenties, you may not have had the chance to develop a unique identity but assumed the role of who you wanted, or thought, you should be. A lot of kids become part of a couple in late adolescence, and although they may not marry, they will break up only to quickly 'recouple' with someone else, a 'coupling' that prevents their real identity from forming.

"Now you have the opportunity to complete this important work. This is a trial-and-error process. Give yourself time to find your strengths and weaknesses, what you're good at, what you enjoy doing, and what you don't. Try new things. Pay attention to how they make you feel. Begin to validate your perception."

It's an attitude shift. Instead of looking at yourself as just half of a whole, recognize that now you have the freedom to explore the whole you, to find out who that person is. Contrary to what you might have thought, a successful couple is not two halves forming a whole. Relationships work best when two already whole people become partners. So pay attention to you.

"Many people feel that when they're alone," says Shepherd-Look, "they're in a state of rejection. You don't want to go out to dinner alone, you don't want to go to a movie alone, you don't want to go to a club alone. You attach a stigma to being alone. But you're not alone, you're with you—someone you're learning to appreciate and enjoy being with. Unfortunately, as long as you attach a stigma to being alone, you aren't going to be able to explore yourself totally. It's difficult to explore yourself when you're together in a couple all the time.

"People who marry later in life have an easier time adjusting to both marriage and divorce because they are more fully developed. Real intimacy, which is what good marriages have, can only be established after both partners have fully formed identities. How can you share yourself, when you don't know who yourself is?"

Even if this marriage is a second marriage, coming later in life, if you went right into it after your first marriage failed, you still didn't give yourself time to develop. You need this time to be alone, to find out who you are, time to experience life without moving into another relationship.

"Unfortunately, the very thing that people need, time alone, is the very thing which probably terrifies them the most. That's why people 'couple' very quickly, because of the anxiety and fear of being alone. These feelings might even be strong enough to hold a bad marriage together. You can, and must, take control of your life. You haven't mysteriously bounced along without some influence on your part, without making some decisions. This time, make these decisions consciously and in your best interest."

One of the most positive signs of personal growth will be your willingness to give high priority to your own interests and pleasures. Perhaps marriage was a series of sacrifices which depleted you self-esteem. When you begin to value your own needs and act on them without feeling guilty and selfish, you will begin to feel better about yourself.

## Suggestions

*Do* be aware that it is not unusual for a woman to suffer from a loss of identity more than a man.

*Do* know that both, men and women, now have a unique opportunity. The freedom to re-create yourself and to become the unique person you were meant to be but hadn't developed sufficiently before marriage.

# CHAPTER EIGHTEEN

## *Changes in Social Role*
*When a mother's no longer a wife.*

"I was married the first time at the age of eighteen, my husband was twenty-one," says Diane. "By nineteen, I'd had my first child, Matt, who is now sixteen. My husband was a real case. Although there were clues, I wasn't willing to look at things realistically. I was determined to just get out of the house, away from my parents. My husband was extremely immature, manipulative, verbally abusive, and just a real scary person in general."

He'd had a rough childhood, and so Diane saw these flaws as a reflection of that and convinced herself that her love and undivided attention would change him into a wonderful person.

"Was I wrong. After three years of absolute hell, I asked for a divorce. Because he'd spent money like water, we had nothing . . . I ended up with less than nothing. I had custody of my son, who was hyperactive and difficult to handle. For the next three years, I tried to get child support but nothing helped. I even had my ex thrown in jail. But, as soon as he was released, he moved to Florida where he was protected from Virginia state laws."

For the next three years, Diane struggled. She had a full-time job, which didn't pay well. Her three year old had problems, "I was def-

initely ready for another husband. I was tired of dealing with everything on my own."

She met the man who was to become her second husband
through friends. He seemed to be everything her first husband was
not. He was responsible, had his own business, was honest and reliable, and seemed genuinely concerned about the welfare of Diane
and her child. They dated for a year, and then he proposed. "I'd
bought a home, under a government program which allowed a de-
cent mortgage rate, and we were cozy there.

"Everything seemed to be fine for the next few years, although I
knew, somewhere in the deepest part of my brain, that he and Matt
had a real personality conflict. My husband had been raised in a
strict home, and it drove him crazy that Matt wouldn't toe the line.
He refused to understand, or even consider the possibility, that
Matt's problems were emotionally caused. He just saw Matt as a
spoiled kid who was used to getting his way. The harder he came
down on Matt, the worse Matt seemed to become. I was torn. I could
see both their points of view. I could even relate to each. I'd never
been a stepparent, but knew that this problem wasn't uncommon in
these situations.

"Five years ago we had a daughter, Sophie. We couldn't have
asked for an easier child. The difference between her and Matt at
comparative ages was amazing. She was an angel. I'd known all
along that Matt was hard to deal with, but having Sophie made me
realize that his problems were more severe that I thought. I sought
counseling for Matt and myself. In counseling it was suggested that
many of his problems were caused by his terrible relationship with
his stepfather and no relationship at all with his father. Also, there
was the possibility that Matt had a chemical imbalance. In spite of
the fact that Matt was a gifted child, school was a disaster. His grades
ran from A to F with no obvious pattern."

As Matt entered adolescence, their marital problems escalated.
Matt was getting into minor stuff, causing them to have major troubles. Diane had ignored things for too long. She finally began to resent the way her second husband treated Matt. "He always spoke
negatively to him, blamed me for his behavior while considering

himself to have been the perfect father and stepfather." Her resentment mushroomed. "I was sure my husband was setting Matt up to fail. He seemed to want Matt to fail. Only then would his perspective of my son be justified.

"When I couldn't take it anymore, I told him I wanted out. He was also criticizing me regularly for my shortcomings. I didn't feel that I could ever have lived up to his expectations nor did I want to. I left with mixed feelings and still am not sure of myself."

They now have joint custody of their daughter, who is suffering from the separation. Matt now lives in a residential school and is getting a lot of therapy. Being separated from Matt is difficult and leaves Diane feeling down. "I love him dearly and want him to grow into a happy adult. I don't know if that's possible. He's been diagnosed as manic-depressive and takes Lithium daily. He is a great kid in so many ways. He's so happy that I've left his stepfather.

"I am working full time, trying to be a part-time parent, and trying to put my life back together at thirty-five years of age. I am bitter about marriage, thinking I'm just no good at it and certainly have no desire to ever do it again. I know that feeling could change, but right now, after six months of separation, I don't think so. I am dating someone, but I don't want a committed relationship, which he knows. I do need to set some goals and try to be happier. I just feel like such a failure sometimes—as a wife and mother. It's hard to deal with. At other times, I'm happy, thinking that I made the right decision. I'm hoping that with time I will be able to move on without looking back. Right now, all I do is look to the past."

Marriages may come and go, but when you're a mother, you're a mother for life.

## Suggestions

*Do* know that setting priorities is difficult when you're in pain, yet you must. When you remarry out of a need to be taken care of, to be rescued, the marriage is bound to hold some unpleasant surprises.

# CHAPTER NINETEEN

## *The Ifs*

*No, it wouldn't have made a difference.*

"I had many second thoughts about leaving," says Tom, "even though I was the one who instigated the separation. I wanted to be 'free' to be myself. But I was scared to death that I was doing the wrong thing. My ex-wife and I talked about it a lot. We went to counseling. We even decided we would give the marriage one more try, and I moved back home. This only lasted about two months. I'd enjoyed my life-style so much more during my months of 'freedom.'"

Once Tom was back home, it just didn't feel right. So he left again, this time knowing that no matter how difficult the divorce process was, "I was doing the right thing for both of us. I knew that we weren't happy when we lived together, and we were happier apart. I didn't want to live my whole life thinking I was in the wrong place, and I didn't want to eventually blame her for keeping me where I didn't want to be."

Now when Tom looks back, he can see that he made the right decision. His ex-wife is happily remarried to a man who, Tom feels, truly loves her. "And I, eventually, have been able to commit to a long-term relationship and remarried this summer. But, for a couple of years there, I wasn't too sure if I hadn't made a mistake . . . especially at holidays."

"I just recently left my husband," says Juanita, "and he's been asking me to come back. I have mixed feelings about that. My first instinct is to stay away knowing he will be as controlling as he always was and that I won't be able to trust him anymore."

Adding to her confusion, Juanita became involved with a friend, a man "who had witnessed my misery and unhappiness in this marriage. He's been supportive, and we've grown close. I know he would like our relationship to go forward, and it feels wonderful to be with him. My spirit and self-esteem had been crushed—I felt so bad about myself. But, even if I don't go back to my husband, would it be a mistake for me to become seriously involved with someone else so soon? Just coming out of a bad situation, I'm frightened and confused."

"Usually when people make the decision to get a divorce," says Dr. Robert Kurtz, a staff psychologist in Cleveland State University's Counseling Center, "they go through various stages. After the pain subsides and they're out the other end, then they may have second thoughts, and they miss the person. This varies according to religious beliefs, beliefs about marriage, concerns that they should have tried harder, wondering whether they will ever find someone else."

Dr. Kurtz notes that these second thoughts generally happen about four to five months afterward. "Now that the legal system drags out divorce for so long, it may be at least a year before the divorce is final, and that's very difficult."

To deal with the "ifs," "Go to someone who can be objective and neutral and talk. You need someone who is not emotionally caught up in it—friends and relatives may have a vested interest in the divorce and will generally have a strong opinion about it, whether they were in favor of it or against it. Also, many people think that the pain they're feeling while going through the divorce will go away once it's over. But it doesn't, and that can cause second thoughts."

Dean Hughson, a divorced father and information superhighway pen pal (you'll officially meet a little later), offers his personal handbook of ideas, "Divorce 101," a cornucopia of helpful ideas for the ranks of the newly, or just about to be, divorced.

1. Accept it.

2. Learn, in the beginning, to appreciate sleep, small miracles, food, and time with loved ones, especially your children.

3. If you are destined to be a noncustodial parent, the quiet and lonely times will be difficult to get through. Keep reminding yourself that you'll get through it, you will survive, and you will adapt.

4. Stop asking yourself, What could I have done differently, if I had done this or that, what difference would it have made? Start thinking about what you can do to make yourself and your loved ones feel better, and what you can do to keep your sanity.

5. Watch how you handle work for a while. Breaking into tears or telling too many divorce stories can cause problems. Pick out a close friend at work, and ask them to remind you to concentrate on work. Work can be a welcome retreat in the beginning when you're looking for ways to fill your time.

6. Become a partner to your attorney. In the beginning you may need to lean on him, but at $100 and $300 an hour, he quickly becomes a very expensive lamppost to hang on to. If you need emotional support, go to a professional therapist. Use your attorney to protect yourself and to teach you the law. Gather as much of the information he'll need as you can by yourself. Save yourself the expense of his looking for it. Tell him you want to be an active participant, don't just assume he knows.

7. No matter how hard it is, don't call your soon-to-be ex repeatedly, either begging or threatening. Instead, distance yourself until you can do some rational thinking and talking. This person is not your friend or support group. Anything you say can and will be used against you, especially if conversations are taped. Don't write anything, or say anything on the phone, that you don't want read in a court document later.

8. Get out of the house/apartment/hotel room and be around people. Limit alcohol/drug use and instead go to libraries, concerts, mu-

seums, synagogues/churches, etc. Alcohol and drugs will depress you. Friends will help you to pull it back together.

9. When you're having a bad day, identify it as such and remember that the next day can and will get better. Identify good days and small miracles, and be happy when they come.

10. Divorce is chaos, so don't make any major decision. Decisions, like becoming a monk or nun, joining the Peace Corps, or buying a new sports car, can and should be delayed for a while. Concentrate on giving loving support to your children, feeling well physically, and sleeping as much as your body needs. Eat well and reward yourself for small victories. If you take care of your body, your mind and spirits will follow.

11. Join a group and help change the legal system for the better. Ask your church or synagogue if they have a support group for divorcing people.

## Suggestions

*Don't* be surprised to find yourself reevaluating the separation months afterward.

*Do* use this time to think things through, not cloud the issue by rushing into another relationship.

# CHAPTER TWENTY

## *Fathers' Changing Role*
### *Distance?*

It's been three weeks since Steve's wife moved out, leaving him with three children, ages eleven to fifteen. "It's not like I'm new at this stuff, I've been doing a lot of it for the last sixteen years, but adding her former responsibilities to the mix has certainly taken some adjustment," admits Steve.

Besides the extra work, the children are having problems adjusting to the changes and have been acting out. On the plus side, his soon-to-be ex-wife and Steve are on good terms, i.e. they have the children's best interest at heart. "When she isn't working, she will pick them up after school and take them to her place. She'll have them fed by the time I get off work. At least when she's able to do that much, I don't have to worry about what they're doing, and I don't have to do all the cooking.

"I can already see that this is going to be a long haul," says Steve.

Even if you are **superdad**, the first few years after separation are usually stressful. If you are one of those 3 percent of all family households headed by a man (U.S. Bureau of the Census 1991), in addition to your children's problems, you probably have to cope with money, job, and housing issues. You may be feeling physically exhausted from juggling so many hats, compounded by emotional strain—and, if you are the "left" spouse, loss of self-esteem.

"At first, I was so totally and continually exhausted," said a custodial father, "I thought I would never make it. I just kept putting one foot in front of the other, getting by each day. With the help of family, friends, and my children, I eventually got back a sense of control over my life and my feelings of self-worth."

If you're a noncustodial father, you have your own set of problems; especially loss, loneliness, a sense of alienation, and the stress of trying to be a parent in the face of hurt children and/or an angry ex-spouse.

"A lot of people look on divorced men as carefree, happy-go-lucky men who leave their spouse for their young secretary. I describe myself," says Dean, "as a man who fought, hanging on by my fingernails trying to stop the divorce, but I couldn't.

"If you lose your spouse by death, there is usually a funeral and people 'look in' on you for a while. When a divorce happens, most people don't know what to do. I can remember the hearty, 'Well, boy, now you are going to have fun' comments that I got. Guess they didn't know about divorce court, custody battles, alienation from your children, absence of your children, and the 'hole in your side' from the loss of your loved spouse."

"I was a very involved parent," says another noncustodial father, "and the thought of possibly losing my son was devastating. I felt paralyzed—like if I sat down, I would never be able to get up again. But I kept getting myself up, calling my son, and seeing him."

Reach out to people—you'll need someone to talk to, or to help advise you, when decisions are needed. Organizations like Parents Without Partners, whose members are experiencing the same feelings and problems as you, can be a strong source of support. Don't isolate yourself. Stay in contact with people and organizations that offer help.

Professional mental health counseling or guidance may also be a good idea. Make no mistake, divorce is one of the most stressful experiences you might face in your lifetime. It is foolish and self-defeating to decline professional help because you might think that only "crazy" or "weak" people see a counselor or therapist. The truth is that seeking needed help is a rational approach to problem solving. Your local community mental health center will provide assistance at a price you can afford. If you prefer private help, contact your local mental health association, one of the professional associations, or your physician for a referral.

In fact, men take divorce much harder than many people—particularly ex-wives—may think. Feelings may even be aggravated by your traditional gender role, which discourages you from sharing your pain with other men.

You miss your family and children. Consider this. You, as a divorced, noncustodial father may have greater adjustments to make in your life than does a custodial mother. Custodial mothers, in return for the responsibilities and loss of freedom, do escape some of the loneliness over the breakup of the family and are somewhat rewarded with social approval for rearing the children.

You, the noncustodial father, however, often retain the financial obligations of fatherhood while experiencing few of its joys. Whether it takes place in your children's home, your home, or at some neutral spot, visitation is typically awkward and superficial. And you may worry that if your ex-wife remarries, you'll lose even more influence over your children's upbringing. (A concern not unjustified. One study investigating children's contact with their noncustodial parents found such contact to be significantly less likely when the biological parent had been replaced by a stepparent or adoptive parent.) You might feel shut out and lost if your ex-wife controls access to your children and if she has a stronger influence on your children than you do.

"After my divorce," says a father of two, "I felt just fine. I got busy fixing up my house, not worrying about being alone, or the relationship I might, or not, have with my kids. In fact, I don't have a clue why some people become so upset."

If your feelings mirror this father's, you're probably wondering what in the world I've been talking about. Do I think you're just confused? No. Disconnected? Yes. Just because you're not aware that you're feeling angry, or alone, or perhaps even scared, doesn't mean that these emotions aren't affecting your life.

"The truth is that men *aren't* the more emotionally open gender," says Stanley Charnofsky, Ph.D., a professor at the University of California at Northridge. "But I do think it's a fallacy to say that men don't feel deeply. While men don't show what they feel, or share what they feel—in fact, I'm not sure they even know what they feel—they do know when they're feeling hurt or troubled. They just won't let themselves get in touch with these feelings, they block them off."

Normal feelings include fear, sadness, grief. But, as a man, you instantly block the feelings and instead show anger, not even allowing yourself to be aware of the hurt. Unfortunately, by blocking these feelings, you hamper your recovery because you don't get nurtured, people are unable to give you the emotional support you really need. "It's a terrible situation," says Charnofsky.

"In many cases, it affects your relationship with your children. For one thing, you don't know how to say, 'I'm wounded,' so you clutch at your children too hard or use them to get back at your wife who perhaps left you. Of course that backfires horribly because the children are not part of your breakup scenario, they're innocent of anything. And they need you very badly to maintain a nurturing relationship."

In that same vein, whenever a parent uses a child to punish or get back at the other parent, it consistently backfires because sooner or later your child will figure out what's going on and resent you for manipulating them.

"I have an example, and it happened to me during my divorce. I was on the phone with my wife who had moved out. She had been living in an apartment for a month or two. She said that she thought she was going to start to date. I was very hurt. We'd been married twenty years, and I was still trying to save the marriage. When I hung up, my daughter Dana, who was eleven at the time, just happened to walk by. I grabbed to hug her, needing to hold her tight. Pulling her toward me as I cried, she started to squirm. I finally realized what was happening."

Men are often in denial of their emotions. If you can't acknowledge the loneliness, the separateness you go through after divorcing, particularly after a long-term marriage, how can you not only heal but emotionally grow to where life becomes even better? Getting in touch with the feeling that something is now missing, will facilitate your becoming a whole, full person unto yourself.

"When I was married, if someone were to ask, for example, if I would like to have dinner on Thursday night, I would think, would I like to? I don't know what I'd like. I have to go home and see what everybody's doing. It wasn't a matter of would I like it or not like—it was, what's available? Now, as a single person I can think about, would I like to? As a single person, I have no responsibilities, the kids aren't there, no wife to consider . . . so, would I like to? I get to decide what I'd like, for me! So my argument centers about our sense of identity.

"As adolescents, we found out who we are by fighting the control of authority, such as parents and teachers. We took risks. As adults, the main task is learning to be [emotionally] intimate. If you don't, you live a life of isolation. The equation always reads: identity before intimacy. You cannot give of yourself in an intimate relationship if you have not yet learned who you are."

You can bounce back, but you must first get in touch with your feelings, create an intimacy with yourself, and allow yourself to be nurtured—a BIG job for anyone.

## Suggestions

*Don't* try to fool yourself into thinking you're doing just fine just because you aren't feeling anything at all.

*Do* what it takes to find and resolve your feelings, only then can you really move on.

# CHAPTER TWENTY-ONE

## *Mothers' Changing Role*
*Overwhelming responsibility.*

It's not unusual to feel somewhat helpless and physically unattractive as a newly single woman. Women from longstanding marriages, particularly in traditional gender roles, may even feel like a "nobody," once the identity associated with their husband's status is gone. Getting back on your feet is particularly difficult. Older women do face real disappointments. You have fewer opportunities for meaningful career development and limited opportunities to remarry.

And what about the added responsibilities the custodial mother now has to cope with?

Teri, a mother of two, is raising her children by herself. "My former husband," says Teri, "left four years ago, when my children were then four and six. He remarried one week after the divorce was final, the woman he was seeing while we were married. It has been tough for us. I work thirty-five hours a week and am just about to complete a college degree.

"I don't feel as if I have enough time for anything, but when I finish school, I will be able to provide a better life for us. All I have time for is my kids and their activities, my job as a teacher, and my college courses. No social life for the time being.

"Sometimes it is lonely. I live in a suburb where not many people are divorced. Those that are probably don't have any more time than I do. I am no longer in contact with many of the people I knew before the divorce. They are all sympathetic, but the women live very different life-styles than the one I now lead."

As a mother with sole custody, Teri has her share of challenges. It is her job to provide not only for their financial support but also for the day-to-day care of her children. "My difficulties are aggravated by discrimination in hiring, promotion, and salaries, by the high cost of child care, and by less extensive work experience and training."

Sharon, divorced after a seventeen-year marriage, is raising an eight and twelve year old. "I find myself constantly tired," says Sharon, concerned that "I seem to have lost my old fun, laughing, spontaneous self along the way."

"There are always going to be changes in roles," says Dr. Robert Kurtz, a psychologist in Cleveland State University's Counseling Center. "If a woman was primarily responsible for taking care of the kids, and now she has to work, run a household, and a lot of other things . . . that adds a number of roles. The woman is usually the one who takes on more, as all aspects of a woman's life change during a divorce."

"I think I am truly going out of my mind," says Gina. "As soon as my little twenty-month-old Noah leaves for the weekend with his dad, I freak out. I plummet into such deep depression that my body feels like it weighs a ton and I'm glued to the floor.

"I think part of the problem is that besides my therapist, I feel that I have no support. My mom lives in Australia, and my father is a total flake alcoholic. I just don't feel comfortable talking to friends. I really don't have that many. I haven't cultivated any because of my emotionally consuming, short-lived marriage, and full time school course. So here I am feeling desperately alone."

Gina is in a twelve-step program and going there only seems to make matters worse. "A bunch of people knew my ex when we were still together, and they say, 'Don't you feel bad about what this is doing to your son?' Oh, great! Just what I need to hear. That spirals into feelings of guilt, and I start thinking, why did I leave after all. I'm afraid I'm going to be alone the rest of my life.

"I am so angry at my ex for not fighting for me harder. I was so unhappy with our relationship. When I asked for a divorce, he immediately said okay—without batting an eyelash—and that's the last we talked. Except through attorneys. He seems to be having this great time, and I feel miserable. I just can't seem to snap out of my depression."

Wherever Teri goes, she sees couples together and her heart breaks. It makes her sad for what they could have had. "I was in love with the fantasy of marriage, not him or the marriage itself. The reality was that he is a controlling, abrasive man, and although I know I probably held expectations for him that were too high, he wasn't capable of giving in in the least bit. We didn't have a partnership, it was a dictatorship. We even tried counseling, but he flat-out refused to meet my needs, even though I agreed to try my best to meet his.

"I guess I just wanted someone to tell me for sure I did the right thing. Is my son going to suffer for my mistake? Should I have stuck it out? Is this how most people feel about being separated for six months? Shouldn't I be feeling better by now? It really, really hurts. I guess if I had more people I could talk to and socialize with, I would feel better. But I don't. My first priority is Noah, and my school comes a close second."

Two months later, Teri is, indeed, feeling some relief. She reports that she is "better, but anxious about the future. My bad days aren't as bad anymore. And sometimes, depending on how well I do in school, I am actually exuberantly happy."

All in all, you may be feeling very much alone as you struggle with money, scheduling, and discipline problems, often passing up chances to meet people and, even if you want to, to marry again. Researchers have painted a pretty gloomy picture of a woman's life after divorce. Yet, many women do go on to wonderfully fulfilling single lives or happy remarried ones.

## Suggestions

*Do* realize you will have added responsibilities and less help as a single mom.

*Do* enlist the help of friends and family whenever possible.

*Do* seek the help of your ex-spouse by keeping positive lines of communication open. Regardless of the divorce, strive for mutual cooperation as parents.

# CHAPTER TWENTY-TWO

## *Custody*
*Creating a new family framework.*

Only one out of two children live in a nuclear family, i.e. a family composed solely of both biological parents and full brothers and sisters, in the United States, according to the Census Bureau's figure in 1991. Breaking these numbers down even more, 7.2 percent of children live with at least one grandparent, 21.2 percent live with mother only, and 2.7 percent live with father only.

"My second marriage went to hell because my wife felt the passion had gone from our marriage," says Ken, a divorced father of two. "As it turned out, she was having an affair. Our daughter was about nine months old, plus my wife had custody of a fourteen-year-old daughter from a previous marriage."

At that time they were living at Ken's mother's house because they were remodeling theirs, which was stressful. His wife started going out alone at night, staying out later and later until it became overnight—"obviously lying about where she'd been. Finally I couldn't take it anymore, I freaked out, and we filed. I was miserable. My life, my daughter, and my home were slipping away. I knew that I had to do whatever I could to keep my daughter. We have a special bond, and I couldn't stand the thought of not being with her."

When Ken first separated, his daughter lived with his ex. "After a few weeks of generously offering to take care of my daughter when she was out partying, I changed my tact and started being unavailable. This was a problem for her because baby-sitters weren't affordable. After a few more weeks, I gradually began having my daughter more and more until finally I was able to convince my wife that since two kids were obviously a burden on her, I would take my daughter full time until her life settled down."

After a few months, Ken approached her with a modified child-custody agreement which has been incorporated in their final judgment. It stated that he would have full legal and physical custody with unspecified visitation rights. He also agreed to no child support payments; and "she has been very good about not giving me any—and I have very rarely asked." His ex now has their daughter every other weekend.

"When my daughter was about two years old, I remarried. My wife was a responsible, active woman with a good job, from a nice family who kept herself and our environment tidy. Importantly, she got along well with my daughter and really became a mother substitute. Looking back, I realize that while my reasons for marrying her were logical at the time, I didn't really love her nor was I particularly attracted to her sexually.

"When my daughter was three, my son was born. This was a turning point in our marriage. After he was born, my wife went downhill, progressively becoming a messy, disorganized, unmotivated person. Our sex life was boring. I understand that women go through postpartum changes, but this was ridiculous."

Around the time his daughter turned six and began to develop a stronger personality, it became increasingly difficult for his wife to cope. "They would argue like a couple of adolescents," says Ken. "It's too bad because at the same time she did a lot for her, such as the Girl Scouts, swim team, etc. But the things she said to her, like tearing down her real mother, negated the good.

"My daughter is now ten, and their relationship has completely deteriorated. She pretty much concentrates on our son while everything else goes begging. We're filing for divorce.

"We are still discussing child-custody arrangements, but most likely we will have joint custody, and my son will initially stay mostly with his mother. I will pay child and spousal support until she gets a job, then only child support. I would rather have my son full time, but I don't think I can make a case as to why he would be better off with me alone. I worry about him. At seven years old, he won't go to sleep unless his mom lays down with him."

Carol, a mother of four, found that their best custody arrangement meant splitting up siblings. "I was married for sixteen years and have four children ranging in age from five to fourteen," began Carol. "As divorces go, I guess you could say that I had a pretty good one.

"My husband and I were both ready to move on. But, even though my husband and I were miserable, I'm the kind of person who avoids change. So I hung in there and hung in there—not wanting to admit our failure. It took his coming home one night and saying, 'I want out,' for things to get moving. The minute he said it, I felt a sense of tremendous relief. I could not have done that to him, but I'm so glad he could do it to me!"

Remembering, Carol continues, "We'd lived in New York until six years ago when my husband came to California looking for work in the movie industry. The children and I were going to follow as soon as he had a job. Well, he got a job all right, he got a job out of state, working on location! So I still didn't join him because I was pregnant and didn't want to move across country with a new baby—only to be alone. The two eldest children were able to join him. So in a sense we were separated, although only geographically. I guess that most of my real grieving happened then. I went through a miserable time."

Finally, Carol moved to California—to discover that her husband wanted a divorce. "Once I was here, I realized, in about two hours, that our marriage really was over. The hardest part was that my support system, my family and friends, were back home in New York. I did nothing but cry those first three months. I called Parents Without Partners, which helped."

Carol was so miserable that her husband offered to keep all the children while she went back to New York to pull herself together. "It was wonderful having time for myself. I came back to California a year later, now we each have two children and live about fifteen minutes apart. I have the two boys, the fourteen year old and the five year old. My husband has a boy and a girl, a twelve and a seven year old.

"The children basically decided amongst themselves who would live where and with whom. Their choice of house was pretty much based on the most geographically convenient in terms of school and friends. The children visit back and forth. The divorce papers state 'visitation as desired.' Our arrangement has turned out to be more like joint custody and seems to be comfortable for everyone. The children are happy living apart, they get along much better. When my husband goes on location, I cover for him by taking all four."

Unfortunately, workable solutions aren't, for many parents, as easily reached or as satisfactory as Carol's.

"Today I spoke to a psychologist a bit about my frustrations with the child-custody rulings I, and my friends, have found," says Dean. "The court actually seems bent on limiting access to noncustodial parents. I don't believe that there is any psychological or sociological study that can justify that, but the court finds that the custodial parent, 80 percent of the time, will complain less if the children are not being shifted around as in joint-custody arrangements."

"The psychologist," continues Dean, "had a very interesting point for me. I told him that on the one hand, I accept what is being done to my children by a legal system which builds 'visitors' instead of co-parents and think that I should drop the gloves and accept that I've been beaten, right or wrong. On the other hand, my activist side wants to fight this thing till the bitter end.

"He told me that he has asthma, yet, as a jogger, when it flares up he absolutely wants to run through the pain. In reality there is a limitation that will probably end his run. For the noncustodial parent, that usually is money and an unwillingness to accept the emotional pain that goes along with reopening the wounds from losing your children."

Regardless of the laws and rights which we all try to live by, answers aren't simple and require compromise. Life is messy, despite the rights our courts are forever trying to define in an ongoing need to protect children and parents.

The following are a few examples of custody opinions issued by the courts. For the sake of clarity, I have taken the liberty of simplifying some of the language, only in an attempt to make the meaning more quickly understood.

- The rights of parents to the care, custody, and nurture of their children cannot be denied without violating those fundamental principles of liberty and justice which lie at the base of all our civil and political institutions, and such right is a fundamental right protected by this amendment [First] and Amendments 5, 9, and 14. *Doe v. Irwin*, 441 F Supp 1247; U.S. D.C. of Michigan, (1985).
- A parent's right to preserve his relationship with his child derives from the fact that a rich and rewarding life is likely to depend on his ability to participate in rearing of his children. A child has a corresponding right to be raised by a loving, responsible, reliable adult. *Franz v. U.S.*, 707 F 2d 582, 595-599; UD Ct App (1983).
- Legislative classifications which distribute benefits and burdens on the basis of gender carry the inherent risk of reinforcing stereotypes about the proper place of women and their need for special protection; thus, even statutes purportedly designed to compensate for and improve the effects of past discrimination against women must be carefully tailored. The state cannot be permitted to classify on the basis of sex. *Orr v. Orr*, 99 S Ct 1102; 4340 US 268 (1979).
- The United States Supreme Court held that the "old notion" that "generally it is the man's primary responsibility to provide a home and its essentials" can no longer justify a statute that discriminates on the basis of gender. No longer is the female destined solely for the home and the rearing of the family and only the male for the marketplace and the world of ideas. *Stanton v. Stanton*, 421 US 7, 10; 95 S Ct 1373, 1376, (1975).

These are lofty ideals, but life isn't lived in a courtroom. Parents may struggle over custody or alter agreed arrangements, but when they do, problems multiply. In a parental tug of war, children feel even more insecure. The sooner you resolve your custody problems, the sooner your child's anxiety will fade.

Custody situations vary, but the optimum solution provides for the best care and welfare of the child. A mother of two says, "My sons are ages four and ten. My ten year old lives with me because his father is deceased. When my younger son was two, I divorced his father. I gave my ex custody because he was better able to care for my younger son than I was financially. He moved in with his parents, who are retired, and they, essentially, have been raising my son. I see him often, and he's doing very well. I couldn't have provided either of my sons with the life-style they have now if I had had custody of both. My in-laws provide day care and a lot of love for my younger son.

"Still, it was and is an emotional nightmare learning to live with only one of my sons. The hardest part is the looks I get from people when I say my youngest lives with his dad. It's as if I must have done something terrible to lose him.

"In my heart of hearts, I know the decision I made to give custody to his father was the right decision based on the needs of the child. Yet there are days when it is hard to get through life knowing there is so much I'm missing in his life. He's old enough to call me now, and he'll tell me about his life. It hurts so much knowing that I'm missing some of it, even though I see him several times a week."

How do you divide a child's time (i.e. love), or separate a family without leaving scars? If children remain with one parent, which one? Will the children live in both homes, in shared custody, dividing time between you?

Try to carefully balance your needs with those of your children to avoid creating any more problems than absolutely necessary. For example, the decision to keep the family home for the child's sake may cause a financial hardship. Or, if the family cannot afford to buy another car, it may be necessary for one parent to relocate closer to public transportation. Whatever living arrangements are chosen, they should address practical as well as emotional needs.

Once the basic plan is made, many other issues will come up, needing to be settled. How can the responsibility of child care and living expenses be fairly divided? Who will care for the children? Where? How? If both parents share expenses, how and when? Who will pay for medical care, insurance, transportation, food, clothing?

How will college costs be handled? How will the other thousand and one responsibilities be shared?

As terms are worked out, no matter how trivial they may seem, write them down. For example, where will the children spend holidays and vacations? Will you alternate attendance at school functions with your ex-spouse? Which parent will provide transportation to extracurricular activities and social events? Will the absent parent's visitation privileges change as the children get older?

Disagreements should be expected. Handle them as calmly and objectively as possible. Each of you has to expect some compromise. Look for ways to see the other's point of view, even if it's a generous stretch on your part. The bottom line? Each of you must keep the best interests of the child in mind.

Difficulties in reaching a compromise on important issues may significantly worsen once lawyers get into the act. While hiring lawyers is possibly the best approach in many divorces, legal procedures typically require an adversarial stance.

Jennifer adds, "When the lawyers became involved in our case, the battle lines were firmly drawn, and communication between me and my husband became increasingly difficult. This led to increased conflict and isolation during the first year of our separation and made things more difficult for our children, also."

"My four-year-old son's mother," says Mark, "has two other children. She has lost custody of both due to neglect and/or abandonment. She has worked a total of three months in her entire twenty-nine years. When asked by my attorney during a deposition, she said she planned to support herself with public assistance for the rest of her life.

"She has taken our son to the emergency room at least three times that I know of; once for allowing him to eat rat poison, once because she dropped him on his head on the sidewalk when he was six months old, and once for burning him with an iron, which she said he did to himself.

"Having been reported to the Department of Human Services about a dozen times for abuse/neglect, once by me, they finally checked on her and found her living situation to be 'beyond description' due to the filth and garbage piled in every room of the house.

"She has been committed to, or voluntarily entered, mental institutions at least eight different times. The last two were because she 'couldn't deal with our son.' In the same deposition, she said being mentally ill made her a 'damn good mother' because she could spend all her time at home, being unable to deal with people.

"For her last trip to the mental hospital, she left our son with some neighbors she barely knew and told them she would be back in a couple of days. Two weeks later, those neighbors called me to ask if I could help find the boy's father since I had the same last name, they looked me up in the phone book. That was two years ago, and I filed for custody.

"When she learned of my lawsuit, she immediately moved, hiding from me and the court. Six months later, we tracked her down and finally got her into court. Her legal-aid lawyer was able to get one delay after another, stretching out the time to over a year. When we finally got to trial, the judge would not allow any testimony or evidence pertaining to anything over a year old—sustaining her lawyer's objection to the 'remoteness of the evidence.' When told by my lawyer that we didn't have anything less than a year old because she had been in hiding, the judge said, 'Well, of course she was hiding, he was trying to take her child away from her.'

"The judge also told my attorney that he would rather not waste his time listening to us because he 'doesn't give custody to fathers,' but that he was not prejudiced against me in particular, so we could not change judges. The judge found in her favor, saying we were 'nit-picking.'"

Mark adds, "I have a successful business and am married to a successful M.D. We have a combined income of over $200,000 a year, own a nice seven-bedroom house, don't use drugs, smoke, drink a lot, etc. In fact, nothing was presented in court as to why I should *not* have custody. The only thing I did wrong, apparently, was to be a man living in Oklahoma. I love my son and will continue to do my best for him in spite of the circumstances which have been forced on him.

"My next move will be to save the attorney's fees and bribe his mother, probably what I should have done in the first place. I know it will have to be a lot of money though. She views my son as her free ticket for life."

Obviously, custody is a responsibility as well as a right. While there are no perfect answers, barring mental illness, custody does not have to be an all-or-nothing mess. There are a number of options for sharing responsibility. Explore the advantages and disadvantages of each—come to terms with what is acceptable in your particular situation.

*Single-Parent Custody.* Neither person relinquishes parenthood in single-parent custody, but it is decided that one should be physically in charge. The key consideration for assuming the custodial role is: Who can provide the best care and developmental environment for the child? Although the mother traditionally received custody, it has been found that children do not need a mother as much as a nurturing, supportive environment, which either parent can provide. Changes in our society have greatly altered the stereotyped roles of men and women. With more than half of all mothers currently employed, fathers are assuming an increasingly greater share of child-care responsibilities, and a growing number of men are seeking and gaining custody of their children.

Still, the vast majority of single parents are women, often with serious financial problems. If a woman has never worked, she may need alimony to enable her to stay at home with the children while they are young and to provide reeducation for herself as they grow older. Unfortunately, millions of single-parent women receive little or no alimony or child-support payments. Two-thirds of mothers with custody must work to make ends meet, usually for less pay than a man. Custody of young children may also mean that only part-time work is possible, which also limits income.

Fathers who receive custody have to learn to cope with problems other than financial, and standards of living also may be lowered. Studies show that fathers may be less prepared for the day-to-day demands of child care, such as taking care of children when they're sick, shopping, preparing meals, doing the laundry, cleaning, and the many chores that keep a household running smoothly.

Whichever parent has custody needs to prepare for additional responsibilities and problems. For a working parent, the responsibilities of a job and child care can be exhausting. Add the stress of being solely in charge—the only parent available to meet the daily needs of the children, and it's easy to see that life for the custodial parent can be tough.

Sharon, looking back on this time says, "I felt totally disorganized, like I was going in all directions at once and accomplishing nothing at the same time. Like Humpty Dumpty, I thought I would never get the pieces together again."

You may even begin to resent the departing parent's freedom and life-style, be tempted to refuse visitation rights as a form of punishment, or alienate the children from your former spouse. Don't.

The parent who has left may, on the other hand, feel isolated and resentful, having lost an active voice in the way the children are being raised. Visiting children at a former home may be awkward and painful—for everyone, especially when it's time to say goodbye. To avoid these bad feelings, you might be tempted to cut back on visits or the time you spend with your children. But absence is a terrible solution in the long run, especially for them. Your visits strongly affect your children's self-esteem. Maintaining a close relationship is important and should not be underestimated by you or your ex-spouse.

Sam, a nine-year-old boy, who showed symptoms of depression and whose school performance began to decline after his parents' separation, described this situation to his counselor: "Dad and I were always close, but now he hardly comes around. I don't know whether he doesn't love me anymore or if he's afraid to visit because he and mom get into a big fight whenever he does."

When you and your ex-spouse are cooperative and supportive of each other as parents, your children are less likely to play one against the other, disobey rules, and test limits. It is vital for children living with one parent to spend time with the other in as natural and relaxed a way as possible. Children need both a mother and a father they can depend on. What they don't need—or want—is to take sides. When one parent resists the temptation to interfere with the child's relationship with the other, regardless of anger and a need for revenge, children adjust to the separation more easily, and that's in everyone's best interest.

*Joint Custody*. Parents legally share responsibility for the children in joint custody. The details can be worked out in various ways. For example, children may live half time with each parent or weekdays with one and weekends with another, or the school year with one and vacation time with the other. While living arrangements may or may not differ much from single-custody divorces, joint custody implies that both parents take equal responsibility for decision making.

The advantage to you is that responsibility is shared; and the children reap the reward of staying closely tied to both parents. However, there are practical and emotional disadvantages. When children are moved back and forth from home to home, they may feel confused or rootless. Joint custody can also cause divided loyalties, an emotional seesaw for parents and child.

For joint custody to work well, you'll need to separate child-rearing issues from your problems with each other. You'll need to work out dividing your children's time between two homes, as well as the energy to carry it out. Many parents find sharing responsibility and time is worth the effort and a viable alternative to custody battles.

A father, who is also a lawyer, reports that joint custody has worked well for his family. "My former wife and I each keep the children for a week on an alternating basis. It's a lot of work moving the kids back and forth, and at first the kids had some problems—leaving behind needed schoolbooks or keeping their friends apprised at which place they would be. But they adjusted quickly and now enjoy the access to both of us. As parents, we also find it easier to share the burdens. Of course, we live in the same community, and I believe that, if one of us wanted to move away, we would have to change our custody arrangements.

*Split Custody*. If there is more than one child in the family, children may be divided between parents. The older children may live with the father and girls with the mother, for example. Courts seldom divide families, feeling that children of the same family should grow up together. In general, it's best not to separate siblings, as older children can help the younger ones understand and adjust.

*Other Arrangements.* Single parents sometimes share responsibilities of parenting with other adults or grandparents so that a supervising adult is present at all times. While shared responsibilities can lessen personal burdens, conflicts may come up, unless lines of authority are clear.

How will custody be changed or rearranged to accommodate the future? Will a parent retain custody after remarriage and, if so, under what conditions? If both parents die or are unable to care for the children, who will become responsible for them? Because it's impossible to know what may happen in the future, it helps to keep the terms of custody flexible so that they can change with circumstances. Or, sometimes, the terms originally agreed on may not work in practice. Making allowances for revisions when they become necessary helps to prevent disagreements and court battles.

Also, the children may want a change of custody, perhaps to be with the other parent who lives closer to school, or for some other reason.

Because renegotiating can trigger old hostilities, many lawyers recommend an arbitration clause in the custody agreement which provides for a third party to settle disputes. In this way, you can avoid court. When flexibility is addressed from the beginning, changes, expected or not, become easier.

## Suggestions

*Don't* think that custody arrangements will work themselves out. Decisions must be deliberate and well thought out.

*Do* encourage age-appropriate children to participate in this decision; however, never put children in the middle of your battles by forcing them to choose which parent to live with. Regardless, be open to their suggestions and needs. Try to be flexible.

# CHAPTER TWENTY-THREE

## *Visitation and Other Rules*

*Hey Dad, just drop by anytime, whenever it's convenient—who needs privacy.*

Visitation should be a joy for all. Often it's the opposite. It feels artificial, at least initially, and it's difficult to exercise supervision and discipline on a part-time basis. There's also that temptation to be a good-time pal, the good guy. These Do's and Don't from Forden Athearn (*How To Divorce Your Wife, The Man's Side of Divorce*) will help keep things running smoothly. Once again, please be aware that while visitation is most usually the man's job, in a perfect society, it would be genderless.

- Make plans with their mother before arriving on her doorstep to collect the children. Arrival time, appropriate dress, and return time is necessary information. Don't handle these plans through the children, especially young children who tend to forget.
- Weeknight visits should be age appropriate. If the children are small, make it an early dinner. If it's teenagers with homework to do, provide a work environment, even if you'd rather go to the movies.
- Unscheduled weekend visits should be planned in advance, especially if you are taking them out of town, and they need special gear. If they've made other plans, be reasonable. As children grow

up, their lives become more involved. It is unfair to expect them to give up a Little League game or a special party. Let them know your plans in advance and allow them to make theirs.

- Longer summer visits offer both of you more time to develop your relationship. Don't treat your child as a guest. Chores around the house are fine. If the child is old enough to have a summer job, encourage and help him to find one. Combine fun and a good time with normal living to help your child develop a sense of responsibility. Let the child participate in the details of your everyday life.
- When your child visits, concentrate on him and his needs. Don't fuss too much over him (he'll get the message that divorce has made him different, that it has harmed him), but try to make him feel that you are a concerned parent. Don't criticize the child's mother. If the subject's brought up by your child, show polite interest—she is a vital part of your child's life. Don't question the child about his mother's life. Ask about his, but not his mother's. Putting kids on the spot makes them understandably tense. Kids want and need to love both their parents.

Are you dating or living with someone? Let their age be your guide. Don't flaunt, either to hurt their mother or to try to impress older children. Set proper examples.

- Do not attempt to ease any guilt you might be feeling by catering to the child's every whim. Make rules and set guidelines to show how much you truly love them. When plans are made to pick them up, show up—and on time.
- This isn't a contest with your ex-wife to see who is the better parent. You are not out to prove to your children that you love them more than their mother does. Don't turn visitation into the Olympics of overindulgence, but do remember their birthdays and special holidays. And, don't allow the children to play you against your ex—everyone loses. Avoid this by presenting a united front to the kids.

Money issues. If you decide to send the kids to summer camp, for example, the cost of the camp is up to you. Don't subtract it unilaterally from your ex-wife's child support. If you take the children skiing, it's up to you to supply the gear. You shouldn't expect their mother to bear the expense of skis and parkas. (Guard against the mother, however, who always sends the children dressed in ill-fitting old clothes. It might be her way of trying to force you into buying them new clothing. If you decide to buy extra clothing for the children, call their mother and ask her what they need.) Keep in mind that child-support payments continue even when the children are visiting you. Most of the expenses of child support march right on, whether the children are living in the house or not.

## The Other Important Rules

Never make visitation arrangements directly with children under twelve. The visit you suggest may not be convenient, and you might be setting up your child for a disappointment. That kind of behavior also tends to turn one parent into the "good guy," while the other becomes the "bad guy." Ideally, both of you are "good guys" when it comes to your kids. So, never suggest visits you have not previously discussed with your ex. It's in your best interest to encourage loving feelings between your child and your ex-spouse. Why? Why!? Because it's in your child's best interest.

Always confirm any arrangements made with children twelve and older. Your ex-spouse has a life and surprises can create chaos.

Send and return clean, well-rested, and fed children. There's no excuse for sending cranky or hungry children, and a sack of dirty clothes, back to your ex-spouse. They're not a twenty-four-hour laundry service—even if they have custody.

Don't limit telephone access between your children and their other parent. However, do encourage your ex to respect their bedtime.

Do not discuss divorce disputes with your children or allow them to hear you discussing your differences regarding them. They will think it's their job to fix it and be justifiably upset.

Do not send messages or money with your children. They're not carrier pigeons and have a frustrating way of losing things anyway.

Do not speak ill of their other parent—or of their relatives, friends, or loved ones. Your child needs to feel good about them in order to feel good about himself. On the other hand, when trouble brews, give a sympathetic ear to your children but affirm and reaffirm as often as necessary that you are not a referee or a mediator between your children and their other parent. But, let them know they can come to either of you at any time to talk about problems they're having because of the divorce.

Do not, under any circumstance, ask your children for information about their other parent's household, friends, income, activities, social life, or dating situation. You will make them feel like a disloyal spy.

Don't believe everything you hear from your children. Not that your children would lie, but things become twisted easily. (However, if you suspect abuse of any kind, appropriate action must be taken.) Don't second-guess their other parent about discipline, rewards, or anything else. If in question, communicate directly with your ex. For best results, try approaching the subject as a question and not an accusation.

Be courteous to old neighbors. Don't honk your horn for your child to come out—especially on Sunday mornings at 8 a.m. No matter what the time of day, walk to your ex's door, but don't go inside unless invited. And when children are to be picked up, have them ready to go on time.

## Suggestions

*Do* let common sense be your guide when situations come up you're not sure how to handle. Put yourself in your child's place, and you'll know what you need to do.

# CHAPTER TWENTY-FOUR

## *Withholding Visitation*

*Playing fair. Kids aren't hostages.*

Never use your child to punish your ex-spouse. Think twice and think again before withholding visitation. The price for that one moment of revenge will be high.

Stuart A. Miller and Mark Price, who are aligned with several fathers' and childrens' rights groups, have put together some impressive data in their recent paper regarding visitation entitled, "Empirial Studies Related to Access/Visitation—With Regard to the Family Dynamics of Divorce, Separation, and Illegitimacy."

In it, Miller concludes that "unimpeded access/visitation is critical to the best interest of the child, as well as the psychological and financial best interests of the noncustodial parent and society in general."

Details of this report can't help but make us pay attention. Too often visitation is frustrated. Consider this. In a 1992 Virginia Supreme Court report, there were 88,375 cases involving custody and visitation. Documents show that interference occurred in an alarmingly high number of these cases, and family courts have not been able to enforce compliance by civil measures.

I have, in some examples of these findings, simplified the language of this important data solely for clarification. Visitation interference is so hurtful when it's used to manipulate or retaliate. Miller and Price show us an ugly reality. Perhaps these statistics will surprise you:

"37.9 percent of fathers receive no access/visitation."

"Between 25 percent and 33 percent of mothers denied visits."

"40 percent of mothers reported that they had interfered with the noncustodial father's visitation on at least one occasion to punish their ex-spouse."

Overall, approximately 50 percent of mothers "see no value in the father's continued contact with his children."

"Unilateral abuse of parental custodial power is more common in court-ordered *sole* custody situations."

"Feelings of anger toward their former spouses hindered effective involvement on the part of the fathers; angry custodial mothers would sometimes sabotage fathers' efforts to visit their children."

"90 percent of the violence and kidnapping we have seen are in *sole-custody situations* in which the sole custodial parent fears losing his or her custody status, or the noncustodial parent kidnaps the child away from the sole-custody parent who possessively blocks the visiting parent from access."

This abstract continues, bringing home the old adage about there being two sides to every story.

Research finds that children suffer detrimental consequences from living in a single-parent household without contact by the other parent. The harm to the children is compounded by the introduction of a stepparent or live-in paramour. However, the negative aspects are alleviated by access/visitation by the noncustodial parent.

"Popular sentiment encourages men to become more involved when they live with their children, but fathers face mixed messages about their responsibilities after divorce."

"Fathers felt their bargaining power to be weaker than the mother's and mentioned the repeated need for compromise and negotiation to maintain regular involvement with the children."

"Few men can afford to legally contest every infringement of the visitation agreement."

"70 percent of fathers felt they had too little time with their children."

"Very few of the children were satisfied with the amount of contact with their fathers after divorce."

"Children who live in single-mother households receive less adult supervision and attention."

"53 percent of children living with divorced mothers and 59.2 percent of children living with remarried mothers suffer from anxiety or depression."

"In twenty-one of twenty-seven social-adjustment measures and eight of nine academic measures, children of divorce show lower performance than children in two-parent families. The results were far more pronounced for boys than for girls."

"Daughters in single-mother homes have more negative attitudes toward men in general and their fathers in particular."

"Divorced fathers reported significantly more depressive symptoms than did married fathers."

"Father reports of poorer relationships with adolescents were significantly associated with teacher reports of conduct problems."

"Only 44.5 percent of fathers with no visitation pay the child support due."

Before you're tempted to slash your wrists, here's the good news. Research indicates that most negative consequences of separation and divorce can be eased for children by maintaining ongoing relationships with both biological parents. Access and visitation help children adjust to the effects of divorce and has a positive effect on children's development.

"The continuing involvement of divorced fathers in families where mothers maintain physical custody has become recognized as an important mediating factor in the adjustment and well-being of children of divorce."

"Children recover more rapidly from the emotional trauma of parents' separation when they maintain close ties with their fathers."

"Paying child support, visiting, and participating in child-rearing decisions are activities that 'go together.' Fathers who engage in any one of those three activities are likely to engage in the other two."

"90.2 percent of fathers with joint custody pay the child support due."

"79.1 percent of fathers with visitation privileges pay the child support due."

"Fathers who visit their children are most likely to have a voice in major child-rearing decisions."

"When both parents share the social and economic responsibilities of child care, children appear to adapt better to their changed living arrangements than when mothers bear these responsibilities alone."

"Fathers have much to offer their adolescent children in many areas, including their career development, moral development, and sex role identification."

"Significant correlations were found between the father's reports of positive relationships with their adolescent offspring and teacher reports of less anxiety/withdrawal on the part of the adolescents."

Whew.

## Suggestions

*Don't* forget, there are two sides to every issue. People turn ugly regardless of gender where divorce is concerned.

*Do* communicate, *don't* retaliate. Your children only have one chance to have a childhood, make it a loving time—regardless of what you are going through. *Don't* make them do it all over again in a therapist's office.

# CHAPTER TWENTY-FIVE

## *Loneliness*
*Maybe it wasn't so bad after all.*
-and-

## *Family Holidays*
*Make it special for you and your kids.*
-and-

## *Pain, Guilt, Joy, Anger, Self-Reproach, Relief, Distress, Euphoria*
*An emotional roller coaster.*

You're feeling lonely. But, in its deepest sense, this feeling has little to do with living alone. Being married can be lonely if you and your husband rarely connect emotionally or even verbally except to talk about matters concerning your children. What could be lonelier?

You miss the warm body in bed, your routine, maybe even the fights. You're sure that you wouldn't be feeling this way if only *someone* were there. Your social life, work, even friendships take on a frantic pace. You're BUSY, but the problem is still there.

Your loneliness springs from feelings of deprivation and loss. Is it

possible you think that your emotional survival depends on every-body but yourself? It's time to build your self-esteem. Flex your emotional muscles as an independent person and begin to gain confidence in your ability to take care of yourself. When you do this, you will begin to dissipate your loneliness, and your fear of being alone. A tremendous freedom is waiting for you.

Work toward an understanding of which needs you can fulfill and those which others can meet. Begin to like yourself more. Stop thinking that moments of solitude are accusations of your worth-lessness. Welcome them as valuable time for reflection and personal growth. See them as quiet times of your own choosing, time to recharge and to understand the changes taking place within you.

A greater awareness of your, and others', individuality paves the way for a new, satisfying social life, one with people in more shapes and sizes than you might have thought possible. When this happens, you won't need other people to validate you or give you approval, you will have the freedom to simply enjoy being with them.

Holidays can be an especially lonely and difficult time. As much as you might be tempted to simply ignore the whole thing because you're feeling overwhelmed—do it for the kids and yourself.

"It was during these times that I wasn't too sure I hadn't made a mistake," says Tom of the holidays. "They were very difficult. For a long time, bad news. Lots of tears—mine. But, the kids seemed to enjoy the result of the divorce and remarriage. More grandparents means more presents and more Christmas events.

"For me, I wanted to skip the holidays because they constantly re-minded me of how a family holiday should look and feel—like mine as a kid, a normal, two-parent family with extended family around for the special event. I knew that my holidays would never be that way again. And they aren't. But, now they're okay. A lot more driving back and forth, but we do the best we can, and we have a fine time."

The two of you and the kids aren't the only ones getting a divorce. The whole extended family is being split. "Problems around the hol-idays usually stem from a broader family context, i.e. if father-in-law gets along well with son-in-law and wants him there at Thanksgiv-ing, daughter is split between loyalty to father and wanting him to be happy and not wanting to see her ex-husband," says Dr. Robert Kurtz.

"I was divorced five years ago, but my husband left almost seven years ago," says Ruth, a director of college relations at an east-coast college. "We had been married for more than twenty years when he left. We celebrated our twenty-second anniversary three months before I 'bit the bullet' and let the divorce hearing happen."

Ruth had regrets. Her husband had been her childhood sweetheart. They had dated for three years before marrying at age eighteen. "But," says Ruth, "I was ambitious, and he was not. He wanted me to take care of him, and I wanted a full partner. To make me want to live with him again, he'd have to become someone else. That wasn't fair to either of us.

"When my former husband left, he was involved with someone else. Our only child had left for his freshman year at college six months before, and my dog died six months later. Although I had a very demanding job and was involved with several organizations, I did not feel needed. The transition was confusing, and I had to do a lot of work to decide who I was without him and without being needed daily as a mother. I stayed very busy and tried to avoid going home until bedtime. I did not date.

"My former husband transferred to another city, six hours away. My twin sister lives there, so at first I would go to her house for the holidays thinking my son could be with both me and his father without having to choose. In the end, it made him miserable. It created so many more 'good-byes.' In one day, he and his wife had two complete Thanksgiving dinners!"

Ruth has since moved to New Hampshire, and it is easier. "My son cannot afford to come here, and I don't go there. He usually sees his father during the preholidays, but spends his Christmas with his in-laws—a couple who have been married for more than thirty years. Now he has a sister-in-law, a brother-in-law, and two cute nephews. I support him in his decision because it is a family, and that is what he needs. The divorce basically took his family away, and this is much better for him."

Holidays are for children and adults to enjoy. As a custodial parent, bring all the joy of the season into your home. You are just as capable of creating a warm and wonderful holiday experience for your children as before your divorce. As a noncustodial parent, your home should reflect this same warmth and attention to the holiday at hand. Don't let yourself or your children be shortchanged.

Right about this time, you're feeling pain, guilt, joy, anger, self-reproach, relief, distress, and euphoria. An emotional roller coaster gone wild. Perhaps you're asking yourself how you can miss so terribly someone you can't stand!

"I'm driving through the fall countryside," says Dean, "in rural North Missouri—where I live. My eye keeps getting caught by old buildings that have fallen. Of particular interest to me is an old schoolhouse. You can still see the seesaws outside and the rusty swing in the yard. The building had strong supports in it, but with decay and termites, it finally fell down.

"It occurs to me that a lot of family picture albums would elicit a similar feeling. You can see the happy days of marriage, child bearing, and then the family falls in.

"You won't see pictures of divorce in these albums. Looking at the old houses, I realize with a start that with a little paint and yearly fix-up, they would have lasted and kept looking good. But the people who've lived in them had to want to keep them going. Divorced families don't have the paint and fix-up anymore—one of the pillars is usually gone and despite whatever attempts are made, the family is weak and falls apart.

"Fallen buildings and fallen families are sad things to me. I can still hear the sound of happy times that used to be resounding in the echoes of my mind."

## Suggestions

*Don't* ignore holidays just because you're not feeling up to the effort. You might be surprised at how much better it makes you feel once you let yourself become involved.

*Do* expect that adult children will have to trade off celebrating holidays with each parent. Talk about it to avoid unreasonable expectations and hurt feelings. Try to realize this has nothing to do with their feelings, or loyalty, toward either parent, it's simply a matter of mechanics.

*Don't* expect your emotions to achieve any kind of balance this soon. If you're on an emotional roller coaster right now, it's okay. Try to be patient with yourself.

# CHAPTER TWENTY-SIX

## *Telling the Family*

*Possibly the worst moment of your life.*
*Owning up to failure.*

If there's anything predictable about telling the family, it's this: It will either be easier or harder than you expect. It's tempting to have specific expectations, yet you know from experience that these people never follow our script. For many, the anticipation of telling parents, or other close family members, is—thankfully—much more painful than the actual event.

"My ex-wife and I had been separated twice. It was no big deal when we decided to finally end the marriage. After all, we're adults. Certainly, from my perspective, telling my mother wasn't difficult. When I told her, she simply said, 'Well, it finally happened.' There was no major remorse on her part. In fact, it was probably welcome news in some respects. My mother apparently hadn't liked my wife anyway. And, as my mother is divorced, it wasn't some sort of shocking news."

Rebecca recalls with a chuckle, "I was terrified of telling my parents that my marriage was over. I guess my fear was that they would be disappointed in me, somehow believing it was entirely my fault. You see, I'd done a pretty good job, I thought, of keeping my problems to myself by putting up a totally false front. Not only weren't they surprised at my news but had expected it. As it turned out, they were more concerned with how I would be taking care of my children and myself than fixing blame."

More often than not, before you formally announce the news, they've had their suspicions. Relatives may actually be more relieved than angry or disappointed. In any case, try to avoid playing out the scene in advance by imagining what they will say—you'll only cause yourself unnecessary grief. Try to be flexible. When their reaction is particularly painful or disappointing to you, if you can accept that their concern does come from love, do your best to focus on the bigger picture, and let the details be insignificant. Find a way to tell them, kindly, what your needs are and what they can do to support these needs.

Your parents, while supportive of you, may have their own fears when it comes to your children and conflicting feeling about your spouse. If your spouse was as close to your parents as you are, they can't help but suffer. They may have felt that this person was perfect for you or was the son or daughter they never had. If this is so, it is harder for them to feel neutral about him or to actively dislike him. They may deeply feel the loss, this empty spot in their family. It would be wonderful if those who loved one another could keep their deep attachment after the divorce, but usually that doesn't work. They can still be good friends, if you are willing, but the breakup can't help but sit between them, in spite of you.

If parents are on the noncustodial side of the divorce decree, they stand to lose more, hurt more, and to take it even harder because they are in the most powerless position.

### Suggestions

*Don't* script your conversation beforehand—it probably won't be that bad.

*Do* expect support and understanding but not surprise.

*Do* expect your parents to voice concerns regarding the accessibility, and their relationship, with their grandchildren if you are not the custodial parent.

*Do* try to understand that your parents are the better for not taking sides and that they may have their own feelings of loss regarding your ex.

# CHAPTER TWENTY-SEVEN

## *Telling and the Custody of Friends*

*Yours, mine, ours.*

"My wife and I knew we had serious problems," says Tom. "We tried talking about it—which lasted about a week—and then she decided to move out, I think because of my inability to act in either direction. I took the hint and decided that I should move out and let her stay in our home. This was partly because she wasn't working and had the time to care for the children. I was working about eighty hours a week then."

Tom and his wife were both very involved in a local Jaycee chapter at the time of their breakup. He was the president of the chapter, and she was the secretary. "When we broke up," says Tom, "there was still five months left of the Jaycee year. The chapter and its activities went on, and the chapter had an award-winning year, but I could tell that the members were never quite sure what to say to us. It was almost as if they were forced to 'choose sides.' Very sad."

In the end, Tom moved about thirty miles away to continue his education, so his ex-wife was able to stay involved with the chapter and maintain those friendships. Now, about six years later, he has no personal contact with any of his closest friends from the Jaycees. "She, on the other hand, went on to become president of the chapter a few years later and even married one of the guys that was a friend of mine from the chapter.

"If I were to make a recommendation to others facing similar difficulties, I might suggest that they—alone, because you could never discuss it rationally between the two of you—decide which friendships are important and make very strong efforts to shore up those relationships. Of course, I wouldn't recommend verbally tearing your ex-partner down at all, because that would further force the 'choosing sides' issue.

"I regret my way of handling those awkward moments, which was to leave the Jaycee chapter and all those friendships behind in my 'old life.' I have a whole new set of friends now, and I'm comfortable with my life, but if I had it to do over again, I would have worked harder to stay friends with some of those great people."

Most friends join a camp, yours or his. Others disappear just because they don't want to take sides. But there may be friends you want to keep, friends who, thankfully, want to stick by you. These friends often fall into one of four categories. First there are the ones who won't let the subject alone. In their misguided attempt to show support and loyalty, they not only agree with your complaints against your spouse but add to them, exaggerate them, or volunteer criticisms you hadn't even begun to think of.

There are those who quickly change the subject, never letting you talk about it. Or, those who can't give you enough advice or let you be alone, even when you want to be. Lastly, there are those friends who somehow are always busy or "just running out the door" when you call. What's the problem? If they are good friends who simply don't know how to handle the situation, talk to them honestly and openly. Let them know what you need (when you connect to what you really need, not just what you think you want.)

Equally difficult, clearly *ask* for what you need instead of demanding that a friend behave in a certain way—a different slant that goes a long way. Such as, "I need you to be understanding when I don't want to talk about my divorce," instead of demanding that this person stop talking about it. In turn, encourage friends to talk openly about how they're feeling with (not about) you—which doesn't include telling you how to run your life.

## Suggestions

*Don't* encourage your mutual, couple friends to choose sides. It puts everyone in a no-win situation.

*Do* understand that close, personal friends will feel most comfortable maintaining a relationship with just one of you, which is a reality of divorce. If you are on the losing side, acknowledge your feelings of loss and let them go. Try to be cordial if you cross paths socially—you'll feel terrific if you can pull it off.

# CHAPTER TWENTY-EIGHT

## *The Family*
### Who are we now?

When you're no longer part of a parenting team, you might feel a need, sometimes bordering on the frantic, to instantly re-create "the family." Struggling, you attempt to force a feeling of family security. Dinnertime, where once there was none, becomes structured to the point of being rigid, "and every Saturday, come hell or high water, I took my sons to the same theme park. They would run around, playing on life-sized trains, while I silently wept from loneliness behind dark glasses," recalls Rebecca.

"When a single-parent takes over the family," says California psychologist Arlene Drake, Ph.D., "she might try to function as both parents and, in doing so, overdo just about everything. It is better to try to simply maintain things the way they always were. Rather than taking on a new behavior, she should try to be there in the same way she always was, i.e. take a moment, get your bearings, and be yourself."

Kids are so attuned to changes that when a mother becomes overly structured, if unlike past behavior, it's disruptive. "Taking into account that you now have twice as much work," says Drake, "try to still be your old self. Otherwise you're overreacting, and the message you're sending the children is that something is horribly wrong, and, understandably, they become frightened. In trying to control, there's the hidden message that things are out of control."

A man's situation can be very different from a woman's. You're portrayed, more often than not, as the bad guy—so where's the emotional support and information you need going to come from? If you have children, commonly you've become the noncustodial parent—which can feel more like baby-sitting than real parenting.

How about a "pen pal," someone you can tell your troubles to—electronically? Meet Dean Hughson.

Newspaper reporter Jennifer Howe writes about Hughson in her article "Linkups Ease Pain of Parting," a story that seems all sunshine but isn't: "Dean Hughson's life sounds like the stuff of daydreams. He grew up in a housing project and worked his way through college.

"For a while, he counseled convicts and alcoholics. Then he went into the egg business. Now he drives a shiny blue sports car—when he's not tooling around in his Rolls-Royce. He has a condo in the city and a farm about an hour northeast of downtown. At age forty-two, he works when he wants to; when he doesn't, he lies on a beach in Mexico. While he lounges, he taps on the keys of a tiny computer. It's a symbol of the sadness he can't escape, even in sunny Veracruz.

"Two years ago, he lost his children in a divorce he didn't want. 'It's the most all-consuming pain I've ever had,' he says. His life with his three children, ages nine to thirteen, has shrunk to four days a month. Every other weekend, he drives to Kansas City International Airport to pick them up or to catch a plane to Arizona, where they'll visit in his hotel room.

"'I was at the airport one night and off the airplane came twenty little kids,' he says. 'They were all wearing those "unaccompanied minor" buttons. I looked around and saw all these guys there who looked like me'—divorced fathers eager to see their kids but already mourning the fact that they'd be back at Terminal B in forty-eight hours, kissing them good-bye.

"For people like them, Hughson founded a computer bulletin board called 'Divorce: Before, During, and After.' It functions as a national support group and has earned Hughson the title 'Dear Abby of Divorced Dads.'

"Several times a day, wherever he is, Hughson draws on his counseling background and everything he's learned about divorce to answer the messages people post on the board. Typical message: 'I've just been served divorce papers. I'm in terrible pain. My children have just been taken away. What do I do?'

"He and the other participants on the board offer advice on everything from hiring a lawyer to surviving Thanksgiving without family. (To find out how to sign on, call 800-695-4005.) 'This does not take the place of therapy,' Hughson says. 'It just gives you a socially acceptable place to talk about something not many people want to talk about.'

"'Hughson often follows up computer messages with long-distance calls to strangers in distress,' says Sandra Doherty, a family law expert in Phoenix whom Hughson recruited to help answer legal questions. 'There was a guy on there one night who was almost suicidal," Doherty says. 'If Dean had not started this group, I don't know where these people would be. I always see notes to him on the board saying, 'Thanks for keeping me going.'

"Steve Borkowsky was battling for custody of his infant daughter when he met Hughson via computer. 'I have sat on the phone and cried with this man,' says Borkowsky, a carpenter in Michigan. Hughson cheered him on in a situation where few fathers prevail. He even gave him money to hire a lawyer. 'More than the doctor in the delivery room,' Borkowsky says, 'Dean Hughson handed me my daughter.'

"Hughson has remarried and says wounds from his broken marriage have healed. But nothing can ease the ache of waking up most mornings thirteen hundred miles away from his children. 'I don't place much value on material things anymore. My battle in life is for the relationship with my loved ones. There are probably ten million guys in suburbia who are upset because they're not more successful, but they have intact families. I've been at the pinnacle of power, but I've been divorced. Who's luckier? I'd say it's the guy in Raytown who's living with his wife and his three kids.'"

At age forty, Dean Hughson's dream was shattered. In 1991, while still married, he "returned from a business trip in Tokyo to find a man in a red coat waiting to greet me. He handed me divorce papers," says Dean, "which tied up all my checking accounts, ordered me out of my nice suburban house, and changed my life forever. I did my best at trying to solve the problems that my wife felt were in our marriage but to no avail. I sadly accepted the divorce and moved back to another state.

"I was not prepared for divorce and knew few people who were divorced—Yuppies like myself were surrounded by either single people or other married couples. Divorce was a nasty word. As most people who end up divorced against their will do, I floundered for a while, but one day a FAX from one of my customers in Mexico City came, and it said 'I have someone I want you to meet.' The FAX had a picture and a story about a beautiful woman who was a psychologist there. She and I began to talk on the phone and FAX each other. We met, fell in love, and we have now been married for two years."

Hughson feels that most people think divorced men are either deadbeats who don't pay their child support or happy-go-lucky guys who marry young women and run off from their families. Dean's story is not only of a father who has had to survive an onslaught of legal battles but of a man who decided to make a difference for others. He knows now that his battle in life is "only for the relationships with my loved ones—my wife and my children. Because that is what counts in life.

"Today," says Hughson, "marks the end of summer visitation with my children, and tonight I will be putting them back on the plane home. My third child won't visit me after successfully convincing the court-ordered psychologist that she is estranged from me and desires no contact. Last night I went for a drive with Liz, my ten year old. She was in a foul mood. Finally she turned to me and said, 'You know, my life is a mess. You and mom are divorced, my oldest sister hates you, my brother fights all of us, you remarried too quickly, I have to fly thirteen hundred miles to visit you. I see a shrink and probably will forever. Dad, why did you and mom get married in the first place—it has created a life of hell for us kids. Life sucks!'

"I cried—still cry periodically when I think of that conversation—and tried to reassure her that the future would be better. But the bottom line was that for her the happy times ended with the divorce. I have to agree, somewhat. Life was pretty good for us. Since then I've remarried and am happy, but my life with my kids is terrible. Trapped in hotels when I fly to Phoenix to visit them, often in conjunction with court hearings that my angry ex-wife has requested, I have little rest or happiness with my children.

"When they come here, it is a succession of angry phone calls from my ex, fights between the kids, stress between my wife and the kids. My children know more about divorce courts, divorce attorneys, and court-ordered psychologists than they do about butterflies. They know more about anger than they do about giggles. Every day I get court papers or bills, or something, to remind me. I quit keeping the papers when they weighed over seventy-five pounds in several large boxes."

## Suggestions

*Do* attempt to maintain old routines as far as the children are concerned.

*Don't* isolate yourself regardless of gender, both of you need support and encouragement.

# CHAPTER TWENTY-NINE

## *School Functions*
*Not appropriate for casual dates.*

School is an important part of your child's world. Here, children absorb knowledge, develop social skills, learn to follow rules, and enjoy scrumptious cafeteria meals. Divorce tears through their school experience just as surely as it weaves into every other area of their lives.

Cyndy Lum, a psychiatric social worker with the Los Angeles Unified School District, offers insights based on her experiences counseling children five to twelve.

"First and foremost, children need a consistent routine, a physical clock," says Lum. "Homework schedules, regardless of whose house the child's at on any given day, must be the same. There should be agreed-on times for homework, playtime, and bedtime.

"Resist the temptation to use your child as a way to get back at your ex-spouse. What does this have to do with school? Let's say you have your child on Tuesday nights. Naturally, you want to spend as much time as possible together, so you keep him up past his bedtime. The next morning he oversleeps—or gets up cranky and tired—and gets to school late. Following a difficult day at school, he returns to your ex's house upset and difficult to handle. Children can't parent themselves. These are issues you need to work out before they lead to friction and anger."

If you have trouble agreeing and sticking to rules, which are ultimately in the child's best interest, Lum suggests you may want to work with a neutral third party to get over that hurdle. Try not to be so rigid that nothing can be agreed on, try to be flexible. But once decisions are made, stick to them unless it's mutually agreed they no longer work, and then, you need to find others.

"Talk to other adults, not your children, about negative feelings you have about your ex-spouse. This is especially important to remember during that first year when you're going through a tough period of mourning. You have many predictably negative feelings, but none should be vented on your children. Find your own network of support."

Do not involve your child's teacher in your battles. "Teachers do need to know your child's home situation," says Lum, "but just the basics—such as when there's a separation, who the custodial parent is, who might be expected to pick them up on which days, court dates—anything that's going on which could possibly impact that child. With this knowledge, the teacher can know more what to expect in the classroom. Perhaps the child might be sad on particular days or can't concentrate well."

It takes about a year to two years for most children to recuperate after a divorce, longer if there are ongoing difficult circumstances. Commonly their grades decline during this time. "Of course," says Lum, "some kids dive right into school, maintaining that one area of success. But most of the time, we see grades decline, paralleling whatever problems their parents are having."

Unfortunately, teachers will sometimes find themselves becoming a confidant to a parent, an ear for complaints and problems. "It's not a good situation," agrees Lum. "Teachers are human, too, and may even have a preference for one parent because when a child's at that parent's house, they always get to school on time, and their homework has been done. But we don't want to involve teachers in making custodial statements, such as who is the preferred parent.

"Parents should talk about what's happening in school, such as what kind of reports are being sent home, to be clear about what the teacher's expectations are."

Handling open house and other school functions may be tricky at first. "Both parents should attend if they can be civil," says Lum. "If not, trade off by alternate functions. After teacher conferences, communicate with your ex-spouse to relate your findings, but stick to the facts—don't throw in opinions, judgments, or recommendations. This is not a vehicle for bringing in other issues; don't use your child's difficulties to make a point or to blame the other parent."

School functions and conferences are a private time, a time to build trust between you and your child. If they're having difficulties at school, they particularly need your undivided attention and encouragement. Dragging along a date they hardly know is counterproductive.

If a child is able to tell you how he feels (without feeling pressured to say the right thing), he may welcome a say in which parent attends what function. "Certainly by the third or fourth grade," continues Lum, "a child might have a preference. For a teacher conference, the ideal situation would be for both parents to attend. But, even when both parents are living in the home, that doesn't necessarily happen. It seems to be a job generally left to one parent. However, when both parents live in the home, it's relatively easy for parents to relate their findings.

"Sometimes it's hard that first year for parents to do this together, but don't abandon the idea entirely because it might get easier. But, during that first year, you might be better off away from each other. The important thing is to maintain communication with the teacher. There are times when parents will need to be called, and it's less confusing when a teacher knows which parent to contact.

"When I find it necessary to work with a family, I've found it easier to talk with just one parent, usually the custodial parent. Or, a child might be referred to me because they need someone to talk to, one on one, to air their fears. This referral might come from the teacher or a parent. It's often hard for children to talk about their fears; as a rule, children from divorced families tend to be more emotionally guarded. It takes a while for me to establish trust, to let them know I'm there to just listen when they have difficulties. I also advise these children to participate in after-school activities geared for children going through divorce. Find out what services and programs are available at your school.

"Just remember," says Lum, "teachers are there to teach, not to be counselors," Yet, where does a teacher draw the line when children need understanding and support? A sixth-grade teacher recalls three different situations when it was impossible not to be drawn in emotionally.

"I had a student whose parents had been divorced for a number of years. He lived with his mother and rarely spent time with his father. Every Friday, my students would take their week's work home so that they could correct any mistakes and have it reviewed and signed by a parent. I collected these papers on Monday to be returned at report-card time at the end of the school year.

"One day I read a story in our local newspaper about a woman murdering her boyfriend. The man turned out to be my student's father. In order for the child to receive social-security benefits, a copy of the father's signature had to be produced. One couldn't be found! As it turned out, the father had, once or twice, signed his son's weekly classwork packet, and I was able to provide the needed signature.

"When I think about how children act out their home problems at school," she continues, "I think about Susan, an eleven year old in my class. Susan was the oldest of three children. Her parents had divorced two years before I met her. Even though the parents had joint custody, Susan refused to stay at her mother's, along with her two brothers. She clung to her father. Her grades dropped, and she gained weight. Her father confided how Susan tried deliberately to undermine any relationship he attempted with a woman.

"They attended family therapy, Susan had one-on-one therapy, but the school year still went progressively downhill. Susan's relationship with her peers went from fine to disastrous—especially with other girls. A very strong leader, she instigated fights with some friends and demanded undying allegiance from others. No one was allowed to defy her, or they were discarded. Many of the students looked forward to graduating to junior high school just to be able to make new friends and distance themselves from Susan."

Sometimes, it's a no-win situation for students and teacher. "There were two brothers, James and Phil, who had been students of mine at different times. James was currently in my class, Phil had graduated to junior high school. Both boys had lived with their father since the divorce; in fact, they had not seen their mother in years.

"One day the principal came to my classroom to ask James to go to his office, saying his mother was there. He was to bring his backpack as she was taking him for the day. He was so happy. My heart went out to him because I knew the real story, and it had nothing to do with his mother. Apparently Phil had been observed with welts and bruises on his body during his gym class. His teacher, required by law, called in the police. The child explained that his father had beaten him with a large leather strap.

"Both James and Phil were removed from their father's home and taken into protective custody, as there was no parent left to care for them. I was not allowed to have any direct contact with either child. Both were returned to their father about two weeks later, after legal court proceedings.

"I let the boys know that I was available to them if they needed to talk or if I could help in any way. Neither boy would discuss the situation."

## Suggestions

*Do* let your child's teacher know what is going on at home. *Don't* involve the teacher in your battles.

*Do* be prepared for some acting-out at school. Any anger, hurt, and frustration he might be feeling can affect both his relationship with friends and his classwork.

*Do* share school information with your ex-spouse.

# CHAPTER THIRTY

## *Religious Functions*

*The new family that prays together, stays together.*

In the fall of '91, after twenty-four years of marriage, Mary learned that her husband, Chuck, had been seeing another woman and that this relationship had been ongoing for a number of years. "I confronted him about it," says Mary. "We talked and both decided to try to work it out. Our talk seemed to help because for the next nine months, our marriage was better than it had been in years. I asked him several times if he had any regrets about staying with me, and he always responded 'No,' while looking me straight in the eye."

Mary thought everything was fine until one Friday night in June of '92. They had been out dancing the night before and had a wonderful time, but that evening, when she came home from work, Chuck told Mary that he still had feelings for Carol and needed to go off by himself for the weekend to "get his head straight."

"I was devastated," remembers Mary. "That was probably the most miserable weekend I have ever spent in my life. I did a lot of crying and thinking and when he got home Sunday afternoon, I asked him what he had decided. He said he thought we should 'separate for a while.' I said, no, I think we need to get a divorce.

"I knew I could never trust him again after the lies he'd told during the last nine months. But, truthfully, the last thing in the world

I wanted was to break up our marriage. Even though I said I wanted a divorce, and started the process right away, I never really thought it would happen."

Mary spent the next few months crying in her office with the door shut, playing computer games to "get my mind into some kind of neutral territory . . . and writing killer letters to him, which I never mailed . . . and still have.

"But I also did other things. A paralegal took care of things for us as there was no arguing over assets. He felt guilty and basically took only his personal stuff, leaving me with the rest. Our main assets were my 401K plan and retirement, which are considerable. He asked about the 401K when I said I wanted the divorce. I told him it was not negotiable, that money was put away for US when we retire, and if you choose to leave, you lose.

"I live in a community-property state, but I can honestly say that I would have killed him before I let him get his hands on the money I had worked so hard for—to spend it on his bimbo. As I said, he felt guilty, and I think he recognized how emotionally fragile I was at the time and chose not to push his luck."

The legal and financial end of things went very smoothly. Mary saw the paralegal the third week of June, and the divorce was final by the middle of December. But emotionally she was a mess. "I seriously considered suicide but knew he'd get everything if I killed myself before the divorce was final. I promised myself that if I still wanted to kill myself then, I would. Fortunately, I've come through it and am now here to tell the tale."

A few weeks after they split up, Mary went back to church. She had been raised Catholic but married a divorced man, in the sixties that meant leaving the church. "I went to our local parish, talked to the priest, and within a couple of weeks attended confession and 'came home.' I think that is the single most important thing that kept me going through that awful time. It probably saved my life. For months, I couldn't attend a mass without crying. Not from grief but because I felt so good about being back at church."

Mary also joined a divorce-support group through her church, and that helped a lot, probably the second most important thing she did. "I was skeptical of groups, thinking, you went, spilled your guts, and left—but nothing changed, all you did was talk. But for me, there was an amazing amount of comfort found in knowing that I wasn't alone. It's my belief that we humans always feel like no one else can feel as bad as we do or be as hurt as we are. But I watched other people come into the group and say the same things I was saying. And, as time went on, I realized—as new members arrived crying—that I wasn't feeling quite as bad as they were and could kind of chart my progress through them.

"In October of that year, I went home to visit family and friends, staying with my [soon-to-be] ex in-laws. The following month I spent Thanksgiving in Hawaii with a girlfriend. I made some new single women friends, through the support group and elsewhere, and started doing things to keep busy. I spent Christmas at home and cleaned house, scrubbing floors on Christmas Day. By then I was feeling good enough to get rid of some of the mess we'd accumulated over the years. I didn't even mind being alone during the holidays—too much—at least no crying or deep depression."

In the spring of '93, Mary joined a six-week seminar, the Divorce Recovery Workshop, held at her church. By then she was coming along well, and they asked if she would be a small-group leader at the next seminar held twice a year. "It made me feel wonderful," says Mary, "that they thought I had recovered enough to be able now to help others. I'm still doing that, by the way.

"Along with the activities, I spent a lot of time thinking, trying to understand and accept, what had happened. I worked on myself that first year and finally came to some conclusions. First, the best thing that ever happened to me was his leaving. I'd been married right out of high school and had never lived on my own. Even when I thought about leaving Chuck, I honestly didn't think I could make it on my own, even though I earned more than he did and am very competent at my job.

"Chuck had had a lousy childhood, which he brought to our marriage along with a rotten, raging temper. The least little thing would set him off. I can't tell you how many pieces of broken furniture, etc., we've had fixed over the years. Thankfully, he never hit me. He was abusive to our cats when he'd be angry at them. I think that's why I never wanted to have kids. I knew he would be an abusive father. I learned early in our marriage not to disagree with him or to argue back when he was mad, or things just got worse."

Mary held her feelings inside, not expressing them at home, and somehow managed to function fine at work. "My personal growth was stunted living like that. Naturally, I didn't realize it until I left the marriage and could begin to look back with some objectivity. People who know me today can't believe it when I tell them how cynical and negative I used to be. Just like Chuck was and is.

"I made so many changes so fast. With my new freedom, I felt like a caterpillar bursting from its cocoon." Mary is now a caring, sharing person who likes to hug everyone! When she was married, she was affectionate to Chuck but not to anyone else. "I took training through my church and now help others, on a one-on-one basis, when they are in a crisis such as divorce or a death in the family. I love the feeling of being able to give back a little for all that has been given to me.

"Last summer marked a year of separation. I was doing pretty well emotionally, getting used to being independent and beginning to really enjoy my freedom. The one fly in my ointment was wondering if there would ever be anyone else for me. Not only was I dumped by my husband, but I'm overweight—neither good for my self-esteem. Then Pete came into a little coffee shop where I hang out, one of those small independent twenty-four-hour places where you get to know everyone and they know you. We talked a few times, and he asked me out. We've been together ever since.

"Pete is the opposite of Chuck. He's laid back and mellow. No temper, no swearing, and a good companion. He's a little younger than I, and attractive, which does wonders for my morale. I know I'm a nice person, but a lot of guys only look at the packaging. Now I know that not all do, and I'm not worried about what will happen if Pete leaves. I know I can make it on my own. I know nothing will ever hurt as bad as my divorce, and I also know I can be happy single if that's the way the cards fall." Good for you!

Connie's husband's problems seemed to have begun in his first marriage. Connie was his second wife. She says, "By the time I was pregnant with our child, I learned the true circumstances of his first marriage and realized ours had little chance of success as it was likely that his failings would resurface.

"After a difficult life together, he left when our daughter was three. Life with him was hell and without him was worse. The guilt I felt at failing in the most important undertaking of my life was so overwhelming that I was left without a reason to live.

"I grieved myself nearly to death for a year. Finally I came to believe that it didn't matter what I thought of the success or failure of my life, what mattered was that God still gave me life whether I wanted it or not. Clinging tenaciously to this hope, I fought off the waves of despair and shame that had robbed me of any quality to my life, believing that God saw a light ahead that I could not.

"My health began to improve, though it was years before it was restored fully. Raising my daughter alone, without her father's help, I was determined not to leave her to seek work nor would I accept public assistance. I took in odd jobs, it wasn't easy. Of course I chided myself—we were so poor. But she learned at a young age to work and carry responsibility. She's twenty now, and we made it. We're now very close, and she thinks she received the best education she ever could have had.

"Divorce is terrible. The hurt never stopped for me. My daughter has hurts I cannot mend. But the wonderful part is that no matter how miserably we failed, I believe that God is still there longing to restore us, making us stronger than we ever could have been before this experience."

In contrast to the chaos around you, religion can provide emotional safety, a place to nourish your spirit. Embracing an organized system of beliefs brings order and structure that can be relied on. In many ways, it provides a form of family—one that promises to be true to you as long as you honor your commitment to it. If you've never been a practicing member of any faith, this may be the time for you to discover the spiritual side of life.

Becoming involved, or staying involved in your church, mosque, temple, or synagogue provides access to any number of potential support groups and social functions; it is a place for helping others, to study and grow, and to celebrate holidays. Volunteer your time to a shelter for the homeless, a thrift shop, or a woman's shelter. Doing something for others will keep you from focusing exclusively on yourself. Working alongside other volunteers is also a great way to meet people and get to know them.

Exploring the idea of religion, and pondering the old adage about the family that prays together stays together, I wonder whether marriages between religious couples prove to be more lasting. "As best we can determine, it does not," says demographer Larry Bumpass, extrapolating from the data provided by the National Survey of Families and Households.

As an example, he cites the survey's findings on marital stability and Catholicism. Traditionally the Catholic Church has maintained one of the strongest positions against divorce among major religions. According to church teaching, marriage is indissoluble, and once a couple enters a valid marriage, it continues until the death of one of the partners. Yet, reports Bumpass, "we find no difference in the divorce rates between couples where both husband and wife are Catholic and couples where neither partner is Catholic."

An interesting finding, however, is that when only one partner is Catholic and the other is not, the divorce rate is one-third higher. Does this mean that shared belief (in whatever religion or in no religion at all) is an indicator of greater marital longevity? "We can't leap to that conclusion," warns Bumpass, emphasizing there are no studies to support such a conclusion.

### Suggestions

*Do* look to religion to provide emotional safety and support.

*Do* involve yourself in social and support groups sponsored by your church or synagogue.

*Do* give your time and energy to helping others in need.

# CHAPTER THIRTY ONE

## *Child Support*
*Or lack of.*
*-and-*

## *Spousal Support*
*Why is he trying so hard to get you married off?*

Along with the decision of who gets whom, custody-financial issues are the most potentially volatile.

Even today, fathers in most families are still the primary source of family income. And part of this income will be needed to support the children, even if mom works. Yet, in truth, most court-ordered payments to custodial mothers aren't nearly enough to meet family needs, and so, many families headed by women live in poverty or on the brink of financial crisis.

Sometimes—surprise—money is used as a weapon when the real argument is over something entirely different. Example? Your ex-spouse might withhold support, or make payments late, or make partial payments just to control you or to show the kids who's boss when it comes to money. Or, how about revenge? A woman who considers herself victimized could demand higher payments in retaliation. If father remarries, which means supporting a whole new family, the problem is easily compounded.

Noncustodial parents sometimes use money to try to win their children's affection, treating each visit like a special holiday, showering their children with gifts, sometimes to the fury and/or envy of the custodial parent who cannot possibly compete financially. Be forewarned. Parents who indulge in financial competition only cause further problems for their children, by encouraging divide-and-conquer manipulation.

"At first," a father relates, "I made every visit a special event. I was afraid that if I didn't, the kids would be bored. It really got to be a strain—for the kids, too. Then I realized it was me and not Santa Claus they really wanted. So I relaxed, and so did they. And we all had a better time with each other."

In the emotional heat of divorce, it is hard to work out financial arrangements that are fair to everyone, but if you can manage to plan carefully, talk openly, and have a flexible attitude, you'll work through what seems impossible—dividing money and possessions. Perhaps a sliding-scale arrangement would be workable; payments from your ex-spouse might taper off as you gain marketable skills and greater earnings. Or, payments may increase to cover upcoming expenses, such as college tuition for the children. You'll need to work out your own arrangement, ideally, with the realization that situations change over time.

What happens when you've been awarded child support and it arrives not at all, in small part, only in months starting with the letter "M," or at the whim of your ex-spouse? You could hire an attorney to go after what's due you. Unfortunately, without support payments, the word "hire" becomes tricky.

Don't let that stop you from recovering what should be yours. Federal law requires states to help families who apply for child-support enforcement services, using any number of methods. However, various states may handle cases differently. Your local Child Support Enforcement (CSE) administration office can be found in your telephone directory under county social-services agencies. Any questions you have about how the child-support enforcement law applies to you can be answered by that office.

Agencies you may become familiar with include:

AFDC: Aid to Families with Dependent Children. Through this agency, assistance payments are made on behalf of children who are deprived of the financial support of one of their parents by reason of death, disability, or continued absence (including desertion) from the home; known in many states as ADC, Aid to Dependent Children.

FPLS: Federal Parent Locator Service. A service operated by the Office of Child Support Enforcement in the U.S. Department of Health and Human Services, this agency will help your state to locate the delinquent parent for the purpose of obtaining child-support payments. It is also used in cases of parental kidnapping related to custody and visitation. The FPLS may also obtain employer and home address information from federal agencies.

SPLS: State Parent Locator Service. A service operated by the state Child Support Enforcement Agencies, it locates absent parents to establish paternity and to institute and enforce child-support obligations.

The Child Support Enforcement (CSE) program is available to help you to: Find an absent parent; establish legal fatherhood for children; obtain a legal-support order; and collect child-support payments. The more you know about child-support enforcement, the more effective you can be in getting information to your caseworker and in asking questions about how your case is being handled. The more you know and do, the more success you'll have getting regular and full child-support payments for your children.

CSE offices are required to monitor payments to make sure they are made regularly and fully. But because offices vary in monitoring ability, it is also up to you to let the agency know if payments are late, in the wrong amount, or if you have received payments directly.

Whether you're attempting to locate an absent parent, or trying to establish and/or enforce child-support payments, the CSE office will need as much of the following information and documentation as possible: Name, address, and social-security number of the absent parent; children's birth certificates; your child-support order; your divorce decree or separation agreement; name and address of current or recent employer of the absent parent; names of friends and relatives; names of organizations to which the absent parent might belong; information about the absent parent's income and assets such as pay slips, tax returns, bank accounts, investments, or property holdings; and, information about your income and assets.

The Federal Parent Locator Service (a computerized national location network operated by the Office of Child Support Enforcement, at the Administration for Children and Families) was originally established to provide address and social-security number information to state and local child-support enforcement agencies to locate absent parents in order to establish or enforce a child-support order. However, the Parental Kidnapping Prevention Act of 1980 broadened the use of the FPLS by allowing authorized persons to access the FPLS in parental kidnapping and child-custody cases.

An individual cannot file a request directly to the FPLS. Only state CSE agencies and authorized local CSE agencies can submit requests. The FPLS serves as a conduit between authorized CSE offices and federal and state agencies. The FPLS conducts weekly, biweekly, or quarterly matches with the various agencies. Each agency runs the FPLS tape against its database, and the names and social-security numbers that match are returned with information. Something like, you can run, but you can't hide.

The FPLS requests addresses and employment information from one of a number of agencies, including the Social Security Administration (SSA), the Internal Revenue Service (IRS), the National Personnel Records Center (NPRC), the Department of Defense (DOD), the Department of Veterans Affairs (VA), the Selective Service System (SSS), and the State Employment Security Agencies (SESAs).

Knowing that time is important, the FPLS is continually working to reduce the turnaround time for providing information to the states. A response should come from the IRS and SSA within two weeks from the date of request; from the DOD, NPRC, and SSS within three weeks; and from the VA within four weeks. If the social-security number is unknown, the response time will be longer. For SSA data, the minimum response time may exceed two weeks. IRS processes cases with unknown social-security numbers quarterly. The response time will be three to five weeks from the time of the quarterly match. Information from the quarterly SESA crossmatches are within five weeks of the crossmatch.

What if you don't have the social-security number? Speed things along by finding it yourself. You can check hospital records, police records, bank accounts, old insurance policies, credit cards, pay slips, or state and federal income-tax returns. If the two of you filed a joint federal income-tax return in the last three years, the CSE office, through the Federal Parent Locator Service, can find the absent parent's social-security number even without a copy of the tax return. Also, past employers or business associates may have the number. Still can't find it? The FPLS can try to find it with the parent's place and date of birth and the names of their mother and father.

If the parent is in the military, but you don't know where they're stationed, the FPLS can provide a current duty station, and much more. If a service member is not meeting a support obligation and will not agree to have payments allotted from his or her paycheck, a military official (usually the finance officer) can have the payments deducted in accordance with the support order. There are limits, however, on the amount of the check that can be deducted. Your local CSE office can give you information on how to start this action.

What if dad (or mom) is in jail? A parent continues to be obligated for support, and past-due support may accumulate while they are in jail. But unless there are other assets, such as property or any income such as wages from a work-release program, it is unlikely that support can be collected while he or she is incarcerated. However, your support order may be modified so that payment is deferred until he or she is out of jail and working.

By the way, it's important to note that your CSE office can help collect child support no matter where the noncustodial parent may live in the United States, or even in some foreign countries.

One sure way to collect child support is to have it taken out of that parent's paycheck, just like income-tax withholding. Most child-support orders require an employer to withhold money that is ordered for child support and to send it to the CSE office.

State laws may also allow: liens on real and personal property; orders to withhold and deliver property; or seizure and sale of property, with the proceeds going to pay the child-support debt. States must also report child-support debts to credit bureaus. It's not unheard of for a tardy parent to bring his child-support payments up-to-date just so his credit won't be impaired.

Did you know that state and federal income-tax refunds may be used to collect unpaid child support? The Federal Tax Refund Offset Program collects past-due payments of child support from the tax refunds of parents who have been ordered to pay child support. The program is a cooperative effort between the Internal Revenue Service (IRS), Federal Office of Child Support Enforcement (OCSE), and state Child Support Enforcement (CSE) agencies. Eligible cases are delinquent cases. If the child-support order includes an award for spousal support, the tax refund may also cover past due spousal support.

For those receiving AFDC, at the time of this writing, the amount owed by noncustodial parents must be at least $150 to qualify for action; in non-AFDC cases, the amount must be at least $500. In all cases, the parent who owes support must be three months behind in child-support payments.

Regardless of where a parent who owes support lives in the United States, his or her tax return will be processed by the IRS through the same system. Tax returns are filed only once a year, so timing is important. Contact your state or local CSE agency as soon as possible to find out if a case is eligible and the deadline for submitting the name and social-security number of the parent owing support.

What if the noncustodial parent works irregularly and is paid in cash? Obviously wage withholding is out, so what's next? Automatic billing, telephone reminders, and delinquency notices from your CSE office might convince them to make regular payments. Other techniques, such as property attachment, credit-bureau reporting, tax-refund offset, and liens might work for the amount owing. If not, your enforcement office can take the case to court for stronger enforcement methods.

What if the noncustodial parent loses his job and is collecting unemployment compensation, or other state and federal benefits? These benefits can also be tapped for child support. Ask your caseworker about procedures, and make sure to notify your caseworker at CSE of any changes in your ex-spouse's employment situation.

What about the noncustodial parent who gives gifts and money directly to the children and thinks they then don't have to pay child support? Courts generally will not allow gifts to a child to take the place of child support and require that child-support payments are carried out as ordered by the child-support agreement. However, in some cases, if the voluntary payment is larger than a normal gift would be, a court may decide to credit the payment as a child-support payment.

Another what-if. Your children are over eighteen and don't get child support anymore, but you're still owed support that was never paid. If state law allows your state to collect support for a child who is no longer a minor, the CSE office is required by federal law to collect the back support. Ask your CSE office for more information.

Fran, a custodial mother of three asks, "I heard that my children's father is buying a very expensive car. And he still owes me over five thousand dollars in back support. Can the credit agency be told?" Yes. By federal law, the CSE office must report the amount of child support owed if the amount is more than one thousand dollars and the information is requested by the consumer-credit agency. The CSE office can report lesser amounts, if it chooses. Some CSE offices now report the amount of child support owed automatically, without a request from the consumer-credit agency.

What if your ex-spouse dies? A well-written child-support order should provide for continued support if the noncustodial parent dies. The child-support payments should be defined as a claim against their estate. The children can also be named as beneficiaries in a life-insurance policy or will.

Collecting unpaid spousal support follows in much the same lines as unpaid child support. Except—you can expect your ex to suddenly take a great interest in your social life. Why is he trying to hard to get you married off?

Spousal support, or alimony, might be paid monthly, in a lump sum paid all at once, or in installments. Alimony may end upon the death or remarriage of a spouse, after a specified time, or certain

other events. Although spousal support is, in a small number of divorces, awarded to the husband, generally speaking it goes to the
wife, and so, to "her." The difference between alimony and spousal
support is simply the state you live in—they're the same thing.

Alimony is based on her needs, his ability to pay, the length of the
marriage, and historically, his degree of fault. It is also possible to
have the amount of alimony reduced by the courts if he has lost his
job or had business reverses. Or, he might ask the courts to reduce
his support if her income increases or if she comes into a large in-
heritance. She can also ask the court to increase her alimony if she
becomes ill, is unable to work, or he can afford to pay more.

If he suddenly strikes it rich postdivorce, does she have a right to
share in this newfound fortune? No.

## Suggestions

*Don't* treat every visit, if you are the noncustodial parent, as a trip
to the magic kingdom of financial generosity. Emotional generosity
goes further and doesn't have a nasty backlash.

*Don't* use money, or things, to try to win your child's affection or
loyalty.

*Do* go after owed child and/or spousal support. If you can't afford
the services of a lawyer, don't give up. Many avenues of help are
available at no cost through the various social-service agencies.

# CHAPTER THIRTY TWO

## *The Quality of the Postmarital Relationship*
*Good, bad, hard on the kids?*

For Michael, building the postmarital relationship is an ongoing process. Because there were no children, the decision to have, or not have, a relationship was strictly arbitrary.

"I don't know about the word 'friends,' but I'm civil with my ex. It took about three years, however. We don't hang out and call each other on the phone to chat, but we have mutual friends and have run into each other socially a number of times. The tension has largely gone away between us. Over the last year, we had a series of conversations about what went wrong with our marriage that were very helpful to getting on with our lives."

Two years ago, these conversations would have been impossible for Michael. "Actually, at this point, I wish her well in her life, but we don't seek each other out. It is also helpful that we don't live in the same city and only run in to each other maybe four times a year. My feeling is that while I wouldn't use the word 'friend' to describe my ex, I can deal with her."

Claire is friends with her ex "in that we are able to talk amicably about things concerning our daughter and mutual interests. Other than occasionally doing something together with our daughter, such as school functions and birthday parties, we really don't associate. There are many things I still like about him, but I don't think it is in my interest, his interest, or our daughter's interest to promote anything more as far as a friendship is concerned.

"We have different friends and lives, therefore our daughter is the only thing I feel obligated to share."

Make no mistake about it. The postmarital relationship with your ex-spouse has a profound effect on your children—good or bad. Don't know what it is? Your relationship has ups and downs, but there's a pattern. Want to see it? Try this quiz by clinical psychologist, Robert E. Adler, Ph.D., known for his work in mediation and family therapy. Answer yes or no. Dr. Adler asks you to be especially thoughtful in answering questions marked with an asterisk (*).

1. I value his/her relationship with our children.
2. I support and foster his/her relationship with our children.
3. I seek to maintain good communication with him/her concerning the children.
4. I seek a positive or businesslike relationship with him/her concerning the children.
5. I show adequate flexibility when dealing with him/her concerning the children.
6. I plan to remain geographically close.
7. I am willing to share decision making on important issues concerning the children.
8. I am willing to compromise when it benefits the children.
9. I make a point of keeping him/her informed of important events concerning the children.
10. I follow through on specific agreements concerning the children.
11. I live up to agreed-upon and court-ordered responsibilities concerning the children.
12. I speak positively about him/her to the children.
13. I act civilly toward him/her in front of the children.
*14. I do not resist or block his/her communication or contact with the children.

*15. I do not criticize or berate him/her in front of the children.
*16. I do not provoke or manipulate to make him/her look bad in front of the children.
*17. I am not or have been physically abusive to him/her.
*18. I am not or have been psychologically abusive to him/her.
*19. I have not threatened or injured him/her physically or through financial manipulation, slander, child stealing, etc.
*20. My primary motivation towards him/her is not hostility, vengeance, or power.

Add up the number of your "Yes" responses. If you have between:

16-20: You see yourself acting reliably and supportively towards your ex-spouse as a parent.

11-15: You rate yourself as acting fairly cooperatively towards your ex-spouse. Specific problem areas may need to be improved.

6-10: Whatever your reasons, your ratings indicate that you are acting towards your spouse in a noncooperative way. Your behavior is likely to be part of the problem, changes in how you perceive and deal with your ex-spouse are needed.

0-5: Your actions towards your ex-spouse are indicative of severe problems in that relationship. The two of you will probably need extensive support, guidance, and help from others.

### Suggestions

Don't think once you're divorced (if you have a child), that that's that, and you'll be able to just wipe your hands of your spouse. You will be co-parents for life.

Do remember that this relationship has a profound effect on your children, both good and bad. It's up to you.

# PART THREE

## A NEW BALANCE

"When A Marriage Ends, Who Is Left To Understand It?"
*Joyce Carol Oates*

# CHAPTER THIRTY-THREE

## *Endings as New Beginnings*
*There is a choice.*

"I felt 'set free' to a certain extent," says Tom. "I have always been a very independent person, even more so with the separation and divorce. I was again in charge of my life and felt I could do as I pleased without having to 'check in' with another person. Of course, I had to balance this freedom with my responsibility to my children which I have always kept in the number one position in my life. So it wasn't total freedom, but I had more ability to just be who I was, and not be 'Sheila's husband.'"

Savor moments of accomplishment, take pride in your ability to handle your new life, which might include planning a new career, living on a different income, juggling domestic and professional responsibilities, managing children, and making time for a new social life. Take a few bows for step-by-step progress.

Toni was divorced fifteen years ago and has been remarried for almost thirteen years. "So I've seen both sides. My divorce was easy, if a divorce can ever be described in that way. My husband and I were good friends who simply decided to get married because all of our friends were. Realizing our mistake, we worked together to find the best way to handle the divorce for the sake of our son.

"Unfortunately, my ex had had a difficult and distant childhood and turned into the same kind of father, distant and without much contact. But we are able to maintain some sort of contact and to be friends. For example, when our son graduated from boot camp, I, unfortunately, was unable to attend. My ex and his family went since they live nearby. I wish I'd been there but was glad our son had a family there to share his accomplishment. My ex's wife telephoned to let me know how everything went, and we talked for hours cross-country."

Toni's second husband, on the other hand, "went through a very sloppy divorce. We won custody of his children even before we were married. The judge ordered that the children were to live in my home. A year later, after his ex-wife had remarried, she took us back to court in an attempt to regain custody. She lost, but the children were put through a very painful experience. She did have visitation, but the visits were difficult for the children for a number of reasons, so we petitioned the court for supervised visitation."

The children dreaded each upcoming court date, so they decided to settle on joint custody, retaining physical custody. "She used this loophole to disappear with the kids," says Toni. "The first time we found them, her husband beat my husband to a bloody pulp. But it happened in a small town and the police did nothing; he was one of the 'good ol' boys.' The children disappeared again and again. Every time we found them, she'd disappear with them again. Since we had 'joint custody,' no court would take action."

After about eight years without them, "the children finally made contact with us and for periods of time even lived with us again. But they had problems trying to adjust to a normal family environment. Added to that, their mother had told them our lack of contact was entirely our doing. We're still trying to sort everything out and work through our problems.

"My advice is this—don't stay in a bad marriage, especially if children are involved. You don't want your children to get the mistaken message that this is what marriage is about. No matter what you tell your children about how marriage is supposed to be, your actions will speak louder than words. And when you leave, don't make your children bargaining chips.

"Even if your ex can't pay support, don't deny the children their parent—they're more valuable than any price tag. My ex hasn't paid since the second year of our divorce, but our son was fed, clothed, sheltered, and most of all, loved."

## Suggestions

*Do* take time to acknowledge your progress at this point and, if so, your ability to have come this far without doing irreversible harm to those around you.

# CHAPTER THIRTY-FOUR

## *Relationship With Ex-Spouse*
*A workable truce.*

Only when you feel secure as an independent person can you be confident that your expressions of friendship toward your former mate are really friendly feelings and not unrecognized hangovers of emotional need.

Building a workable relationship with your ex starts between you and you. You will reach the point of needing to look back and take stock. Chris Archambault (*Divorce Recovery*) calls this process "doing an emotional postmortem" of the marriage. It won't get you and your spouse back together again, points out Archambault, but it will help you settle in your own mind some of the issues the divorce raised.

The first big question is, "How did I get here?" Pieces of the puzzle include: How did I reach the point when divorce was inevitable? When did our marriage really start to unravel? Could this divorce have been predicted long ago? Why did I attract this particular person into my life in the first place, and what does that say about me? What's the real, underlying reason our life together didn't work anymore? How, and why, did we stop being happy with each other? How much of the breakup was my spouse's fault, and how much was mine? What personal issues do I have to resolve to make sure I don't get into this situation again?

When you've sorted this out, you're ready to feel comfortable, once again, as part of a parenting team, to work cooperatively for the welfare of your children instead of doing it just because you have to. If there are no children, you're finally ready to move on with your life. Which doesn't mean that you won't find yourself running into one another socially. Although sometimes, your ability to be socially civil is a simple matter of timing.

"My ex and I have ended up at some parties, but we'd just say hello and go about our business," says R. Thomas Berner, a professor at the Pennsylvania State University and author of *Parents Whose Parents Were Divorced*. "I did, however, boycott my best friend's wedding. His wife, new to town, invited my ex to their wedding reception, which was the day we were going into court to debate the judge's alimony decision. I wasn't in a civil mood then. Now it wouldn't matter. I think my friend's wife just showed lousy judgment."

Without the ongoing pressure of dealing with children in relationship to your ex, couples seem to be clearer about what, if any, friendship is possible, or even wanted, after the dust has cleared. "Not all divorces are fractious," says Clark. "My wife left me because she had decided the marriage was over, apparently a year and a half earlier, but somehow she neglected to mention it. From my point of view, the marriage was over because there's no point going on when one person is no longer willing to make the effort to keep things together. Obviously, counseling only works when there is effort on both sides."

"In any case," says Joyce, "we had no children, we've divided our property, and while we're only speaking to each other when necessary, I don't think there's any anger that needs venting. Dragging ex-couples like us into some hellish showdown just because some divorces are horrific would be cruel and unusual punishment, since we've divided the property and gone our separate ways.

"Initially the shock was horrible for me. I'm not even remotely happy with the situation, but facing off when all the issues are re-solved save the divorce itself would not be constructive."

## Suggestions

*Do* take a good look back, come to terms with your contribution to the breakup of your marriage. If not, you are going to repeat the same scenario with someone new.

*Do* work together as a parenting team.

*Don't* use parenting as a means to get back at your ex or to cling to the past.

# CHAPTER THIRTY-FIVE

## *Relationships With Grandparents , Former In–Laws, and Family*
*Kids only?*

"Shortly after my eighty-two-year-old grandmother-in-law was told about her favorite grandson and I separating, and the real reason why, his infidelity, she wrote to say that I would always be part of her family, regardless of the divorce," remembers Susan. "She said that she loved me just like one of her own grandchildren. Her letter made me cry—it was so sweet and special to me."

Later, at the family Christmas gathering, which Susan's ex did not attend, "I made it known that I would start dating again because, as far as I was concerned, I was already single. She gave a big smile, put her fist in the air and said, 'Good for you!' She honestly thinks it's wonderful that I've been able to get on with my life as well as I have."

Marriage is a public announcement of joined lives which includes your extended family and friends. Divorce shatters this social network. This period is confusing as old relationships are sorted and re-worked. Handled badly, layers of disappointment and bitterness add to the mix.

"My mother-in-law became absolutely frantic, afraid that I wouldn't talk to her anymore—I've been like one of her own kids for the past twelve years, and we've become very close," says Judith. "The funny part is that she's the one advocating that I get out and start dating again. Her exact words were, 'Well, a roll in the sack with a cute, young guy might be kind of fun.' I just about fell out of my chair when I heard that!

"I always knew that she was 'different,' but I had no idea how much until that conversation! She hopes that we can still be good friends, but I think I need to ease into that relationship. I'm still floored that she's suggesting I should be unfaithful to her son. Could she be fishing for information to help him with his case? That conversation has certainly left me feeling uncomfortable.

"Just in case, I'm keeping my social life to myself. My marriage isn't legally over, and although I have my ex's blessing to go out, I'm not about to do anything rash until the ink is dry. Life will be far less complicated that way."

Divorce is so common today that most extended families find themselves touched by it, in both positive and negative ways. While some grandparents justifiably fear losing touch with their grandchildren, others become closer as grandchildren seek emotional support. According to researchers and therapists, these relationships work best when family members resist the temptation to take sides in the divorce, making their primary concern the children.

"My beloved mother-in-law," relates Deborah, "has been very supportive of me during the divorce and its aftermath. She actually found out about it when she called to ask what we would like for our twenty-fifth wedding anniversary, and I was unable to speak.

"But she has been very clear about not discussing the 'details' of the divorce, by which she means anything at all about the proceedings, insults, his failure to pay college tuitions as agreed in the settlement, etc. She wants very much to remain supportive of her son, and she has to remain ignorant of his behavior in order to do so. That was hard for me to accept, because over the years she had become as close or closer than my own mother, and I lost her support and confidence. But I have to accept that she can do only what she can do. And I know that her son does need her wisdom.

"My former husband initiated the divorce. It was a shock to me: I knew he was very quiet, I thought he was worried about his new job, but it turns out he was spending his free time with his current wife. He seems to feel very threatened and injured by me—as though the pain of the divorce were my fault exclusively. I think that he believes his mother's friendship with me is some kind of attack on him, so we've been sneaking around behind his back.

"It is very difficult to try to keep up lifelong friendships rather than splitting the friends and relatives along with the property into 'his' and 'hers.' But I think it is important to do so. I always thought she would live with us when she needed to stop living on her own. Well, some things can't happen as we had hoped . . . "

Grandparents have the opportunity to play an important role in their grandchild's life, especially if their marriage is still intact. To grandchildren, grandparents represent the continuity of generations and living proof that relationships can be lasting, reliable, and dependable. Grandparents also convey a sense of tradition and a special commitment to the young that extends beyond a child's own parent.

A grandparent's encouragement, friendship, and love has special meaning for children of divorce. Children who can rely on their extended families are blessed because their world is a more stable, predictable place.

In 1980 Judith S. Wallerstein and Jean Berlin Kelly studied 131 children of all ages of divorced families in the Chicago area who agreed to participate in a six-week counseling program. Nine worry-questions were found to be common to most of the children. Dorothy Weiss Gottlieb, Inez Bellow Gottlieb, and Marjorie A. Slavin, M.S. W., suggest these responses for concerned grandparents in their book, *What to Do When Your Son or Daughter Divorces*. Keeping in mind that your comments should be geared to the child's age:

1. *"Who will take care of me?"* Grandparents can, at intervals or for a period of time. Adolescents need a kind of baby-sitting, too.
2. *"Is there anything in the world reliable and predictable?"* Grandparents should make a special effort to be there for children as

promised, every time, barring emergencies. When a grandparent says they're going to pick them up or meet them, they must get there and on time. Their reliability is crucial.

3. *"Are my parents crazy?"* When the opportune moment arises, a grandparent can explain what an unsettling period this is for both parents and that after a while, they and you will settle down more and more.

4. *"Where is my father/mother now living?"* Grandparents should encourage visits to the absent parent's home if that meets with your plans. A child wants to touch this new base in order to feel part of his new setting.

5. *"Will my mother/father—my only parent—get sick, hit by a car, or worse?"* Grandparents can't promise this won't happen but can let grandchildren know that they are a backup, as are the cousins, uncles, and aunts from both sides of the family.

6. *"Will we have enough money now?"* Grandparents can reassure a grandchild that he or she will be taken care of. Grandparents can help with money or gifts, giving a weekly allowance or money for a class trip.

7. *"Will I have to change schools now?"* Children can be told truthfully that many remain where they are and attend the same school. However, if change is in the wind, a grandparent can research the positives in the new school and, perhaps, visit the classroom.

8. *"Will I have to move to a new neighborhood?"* A grandparent can recount stories of the times they moved, their new room, new friends, and the yard for a dog. They can offer reassurance that old friends can visit and stay overnight.

9. *"Is mom going to marry Bob? Will they keep me with them?"* Grandparents probably can't do much about this except wonder with the children.

A child may never directly voice these particular doubts to their grandparents but instead may act out their worries by beating up a best friend or withdrawing into isolation from friends and family.

While some children make a beeline to their grandparent's home and arms, others may withdraw and refuse to accept a grandparent's solace. Why? First, their need for secrecy. Not even grandparents can be told about all the strife, the yelling, the threats they have witnessed. If children don't say it with words, the nightmare (divorce) might not be true. Once the words are out, the breakup becomes a threatening reality.

Second, is the misplaced guilt they might feel about having caused the separation. He may think his disobedience, or his four-letter words that infuriated his parents, might have driven them apart. This kind of guilt can keep your grandchild feeling unworthy or unclean, and he may keep his distance from you.

Third is the strong sense of loyalty a child feels. A child may feel that any movement toward a grandparent could be interpreted to mean that he or she sides with the grandparent's child. To risk losing either mom or dad is too frightening. Moving toward you might cause the other parent (your ex-law) to punish your child, your grandchild, or you.

Fourth is the fear of abandonment. Your grandchild must hold tightly to both parents, not let them out of his sight, or one might disappear forever. No one else will do for a while.

Studies show that women are more likely than men to maintain a relationship with their in-laws after the divorce, especially if the relationship had been close—and, if the in-laws approve of the divorce. Relationships between former in-laws are more likely to continue when children are involved. Still, relationships between former in-laws frequently deteriorate or vanish.

One study found that close relationships are most likely with paternal relatives when there's a need to keep in touch in order to see grandchildren living with custodial mothers. When fathers have custody, they are also more likely to have contact with their former spouse's extended family. Surprising, the most commonly retained tie was found to be between a grandmother and her former daughter-in-law. (Also, grandmothers who are divorced or widowed or in a remarriage are more likely to be in an expanded kin system than those in an intact first marriage.)

After your divorce, you may find your relationship with your own parents changed. According to one study, parents interviewed rarely viewed their relationship with their divorced child with the sentimentality they bestowed on their role as grandparents. Your relationship with your parents might even become somewhat strained or tense. With divorce, you could find yourself wanting to become dependent on them once again—needing to wrap yourself in an emotional, financial, or physical cocoon.

Both you and your parents may have to rethink your expectations of each other. Don't be surprised if your parents aren't overjoyed at finding themselves in this situation, i.e. having to give more of themselves than they had expected to do at this stage of their life. It's conceivable that you'll feel your parents should be available to help with your emotional problems—more than they feel is appropriate. Or, just the opposite. Forced back into a parenting role, your parents might become too intertwined, too controlling in your life—even if they didn't initially criticize your decision to divorce.

The bottom line? The Catch-22? While you probably don't want your parents to interfere or challenge your child-rearing abilities or to offer unsolicited advice, they might feel they have a need (no, the right) to voice their concerns. Talk about it. You'll reach a workable understanding.

Saying good-bye to your ex's extended family, people you probably won't be seeing again (but your children might) can be tricky, but it doesn't have to create even more problems. A door closed gently, and with care, can be reopened—a door slammed shut is more likely to jam. And so are feelings. Good-bye letters go beyond the practical, they are the emotionally generous thing to do—an especially important gesture since you probably aren't feeling particularly generous these days when it comes to your feelings. A warm letter of good-bye, without blame or name calling will help you find emotional closure in a way that you can feel good about. You're not just divorcing your mate, you're divorcing a family. All it takes is a few lines to let each know how special you think they are and that they will be missed.

This letter from Pamela to an aunt of her ex is a wonderful example. It reads:

*Dear Gwen:*

*Writing this letter seems especially difficult. You are one of the people in Ray's family I have felt the closest to, and the loss of our relationship is a painful one. I feel we connected in a genuine way, and I am sorry that we will not get the opportunity to know each other better.*

*I want to thank you for your kindness and love which has always meant a lot to me. You are a uniquely caring individual with terrific daughters. I will miss you in my life and am grateful for the bit of time I had to know you.*

*You are a tremendous strength in Ray's life, and I take comfort in knowing you are there for him. My best to you and Theresa and Tracy always.*

*With much love,*
*Pamela.*

## Suggestions

*Do* have patience with your parents. Your relationship may be confusing as they tend to be overprotective, forgetting you're an adult, capable of independence.

*Do* encourage your ex-in-laws to maintain a strong relationship with their grandchildren. Your children now need their entire family more than ever. From your child's perspective, this set of grandparents, along with your parents, are still family.

*Do* say good-bye to extended family on your ex-husband's side in a thoughtful and caring way. Their lives have also been touched by this divorce, and they will need closure to end their relationship, or hopefully, maintain a new friendship with you.

# CHAPTER THIRTY-SIX

## *Starting Over*
*Who knows, life might even get better.*

"I began to heal when I decided to live for me, to like and love myself," says Charlene. "Until I could let go, the pain was there constantly. I know now that I couldn't let go because it was easier to hold on to the familiar than to face the uncertain.

"I now approach each day with enthusiasm, able to make my own decisions, even whether I will again choose to be in a relationship. I have control over how I approach a situation and of my emotions."

When it is your choice to leave a marriage, you have the least pain, if you are left you have the most pain. "Regardless," says Charlene, "you must take the time to heal. No longer am I looking for someone to take away my pain, just as I will never again allow someone to take away who I am. I'm facing life head on. I no longer blame myself for losing someone I once loved so much. I can accept the fact that I had lost the 'me' in our 'we.'"

Charlene learned that she couldn't change the people around her, but by working on herself, she was surprised to see how fast other people were able to accommodate her needs.

"Life is great, but only by experiencing it did I grow. If, for some reason my next relationship doesn't last, at least I have me to hang on to. I no longer feel I have to change who I am to attract a partner.

I think with my head, but trust my gut instinct. If something seems bad or wrong in the least way, I don't do it. Life is such a mystery. Who I am and what I want has been a long and sometimes painful discovery.

"Losing me was my ex's loss. I'm glad to have known him, and I now wish all the best for him—but I wish more for me. I'm glad things happened the way they did because I wouldn't be where I am today if they hadn't."

If you look at any wound, part of the healing process is discomfort. "People," says Dr. Kurtz, of Cleveland State University's Counseling Center, "hate pain and want to avoid it. They can't stand confronting the thought that they did anything wrong. But there's no rebuilding without doing some serious introspection. Some people come out stronger and wiser, but divorce is almost always stressful."

"Last night, while sitting on the deck of my farm overlooking the lake," Dean muses thoughtfully, "I thankfully realized that the 'me' I have now, is not much different than the old one, before divorce. Although I'm more concerned about old age than I was, and keeping my health, I think about my kids and their well-being. I think about friends and my relationships. I cherish the love I get from my wife and friends, the sunsets over the lake, my trusty Anatolian shepherds. I guess that I cherish smaller things than I used to—like the smell of my aftershave and the taste of an occasional gin and tonic. I love those giddy silly times when I laugh without reserve and when my throat hurts from giggling. I love the times when I realize that I love life, despite its painful times. I especially love those times when I can look in the mirror and say 'You sly Devil, you have survived.'

"Most of all there is a sense of acceptance of life as an ongoing work, I am no longer running desperately. Material possessions have failed me, no matter what car, painting, house, trip, thing that I own, in the scheme of things, they are not much in making me feel happy. I am downsizing my life and learning to live on less, enjoying more what I have without worrying about what I don't have."

Surviving divorce felt, to Dean, like surviving a fire. At first it left only scorched earth, "but the grass is coming back. My heart has a few scars, I wish my divorce had never happened, but it did. I think

I have grieved long enough for the love I lost and my old life. My new wife, Yoly, is indeed the love of my life. We've built a beautiful house on my family farm, the one my grandfather had bought in 1865, and we live a gentle, peaceful life. I can hardly wait to get up in the mornings to see what adventures the two of us will have. I have had the pleasure of getting involved in human-rights issues and the inequalities noncustodial people face.

"Going toward love was my best move. I am married to a wonderful person. Divorce may have been my worst move, but out of it grew my love with Yoly. Together we have learned to trust again."

## Suggestions

*Do* realize discomfort is a normal part of your healing and growing process. Discomfort means you are on the right track.

*Do* use this discomfort to realize personal changes need to be made and begin to make them one day at a time.

*Don't* use your discomfort as an excuse for hurting anyone.

# CHAPTER THIRTY-SEVEN

## *Relationship With Former Friends— Withdrawal*

*One—rallying to your side. Two—envy, admiration, curiosity, fear (of divorce as a communicable disease). Three—gone.*

Important changes in your life generally bring about a shift in your network of friends. When you were first married, "couple friends" became the priority, sometimes replacing your old single friends. Old friends should be treasured and held dear; sadly this isn't always the reality. Divorce may also bring a physical move, a change of communities.

Part of the loneliness of divorce is losing "couple friends," possibly former in-laws, even an entire extended family. According to one study, the odds are against keeping friendships intact. Three-quarters of the women in this study reported losing friends during or after the divorce.

After the separation, you may feel uncomfortable with friends who are still married because activities revolve around being a pair. Or, your old married friends may find that your divorce challenges them to take another look at their own marriage—and, you become uncomfortable to be around. Also, couple friends may feel awkward, (mistakenly) thinking they need to become embroiled in conflicts over allegiances. Friends may also be going through their own sense of loss and grief. Different reasons, but the outcome's the same—they're gone, leaving you feeling even lonelier.

In a very practical sense, time can also play a role. This is especially true of same-sex friendships, which become difficult simply because the time you have available may no longer mesh with theirs. Example? You have Sunday afternoons free while the kids are with their dad, but for your married friend, Sundays are still an important family time.

As if you didn't have enough to think about and do, like it or not, new friends need to be made—you need an adult support system. At a time when you're feeling the most vulnerable and incapable of connecting with another living being, it can be especially difficult. However, new friendships can come not only from rejection, or the awkwardness in old friendships, but a positive need for friends to share your new concerns and feelings. Organizations, such as Parents Without Partners, offer support and friendships with other men and women in the same boat. When the time is right, your social priorities may also embrace dating.

### Suggestions

*Do* remember that, in general, old "couple" friends are uncomfortable maintaining friendships with you and your ex.

*Do* make an effort to make new friends through support groups, organizations, your children's school, etc. You owe it to yourself to have supportive friends whose loyalties aren't torn.

# CHAPTER THIRTY-EIGHT

## *Ex-Spouse As Present Lover*
### *Staying stuck. Get a life!*

I couldn't have put it better. "Other than dating your mom, dating your ex-wife seems like one of the creepier social options available," says life-style columnist, Judy Markey, in her (Los Angeles) *Daily News* column.

"When you go to so much trouble and expense to unlink from someone, why on earth would you link back up? And yet this week, I've talked to several ex-spouses who have been dating each other for years—despite raised eyebrows, confused families, and exasperated friends."

Markey begins with Chuck.

"'I don't care what anyone thinks,' says Chuck, a forty-six-year-old businessman. 'I've been dating my ex-wife for the past three years. This was a third marriage for us both, but we only lasted seven years, and that upset us both a lot. We don't live in the same city anymore, but I see her plenty. I guess she continues to be the woman in my life, because I haven't had a date with anyone else this whole time.'"

Next comes Andy.

"Andy has a different deal. 'When my ex and I split up, it was real bitter. We'd been married twenty-three years, and for the first ten years after we broke, we had nothing to do with each other—nothing. Now, I'd say for the past six years, I go out with her once a week. We go to dinner or a movie or even travel. It's not high romance, but it's pleasant. We even have sex. But I'll tell you, it's still pretty much like married sex. I think the big difference now is that we are both a lot more tolerant. I enjoy her company—up to a point. But when I reach that point, I get to walk. She gets grumpy, and I drive her home and say goodnight.'"

Next comes Chuck's ex-wife, Diane.

"Chuck's ex-wife, Diane, feels that he is her best friend. 'Even though we don't live in the same city, I don't think we've gone more than a month or so without talking. When he comes into town to see his family, I always pick him up at the airport. I call him if I have a problem.'

"Chuck, of course, is worried that he may never get over Diane. 'On one hand—the theoretical hand, at least—I honestly believe that a divorce decree and a marriage license don't mean much of anything. It's just a piece of paper, and if two people have a bond, a marriage or a divorce shouldn't add or detract from that bond. The bond is what it is.

"'On the other hand—the reality hand—there is a major difference. Because dating her IS different from being married to her. It's both easier and more painful. It's easier because now I'm not hurt that I don't come first—I mean we're divorced, so now I don't expect to. But it's more painful because now she can go out with other men, and that's hard for me. I don't blame her. I know she's entitled, but I don't have to like it.'

"So then one poses the obvious question. If you don't like it, why don't you do something about it? And Chuck's answer is, 'I would but I'm not always sure what I want to do. And I bet that is true for other people who might be dating their exes. It's like you don't think you will ever get back together, but you don't know what it will take to ever get you really apart.'"

Hopefully, Chuck, Andy, and Diane haven't brought babies into this world who are, if by nothing more than their example, condemned to a future as confused and terrorized of commitment as they.

### Suggestions

*Don't* date your ex if you want to grow and move on with your life.

*Do* think about the possibility that while dating your ex might be safe to the commitment-terrified, there's a hefty price to be paid for clinging to your phobia—intimacy.

# CHAPTER THIRTY-NINE

## *Maintaining Communication With Kids*

*Even when they're at his or her house. Even when his or her new significant other answers. Call.*

"My ex-wife and I have joint custody," says Tom, "so for the first couple of years, she had the kids four days a week, and I had them three. When they became old enough to start school, we had to change the arrangement, so I lost a day and only got them on week-ends. I lived about a half hour away. Then, when my ex-wife remarried, she said it wasn't fair for me to have the kids every weekend, so now I only get them every-other weekend. This is very hard. I miss them so much because it's twelve days between visits. Sometimes they grow a lot during that time."

During the school year, Tom often sees the children in the middle of that twelve-day period when he goes to a school play or attends a football-team practice or helps out with parent-student day, etc. During the summer, he has them for two weeks, and at the Christmas holiday he has them for a week.

"I try hard to never say anything bad about their mother or her husband to the kids. If they complain about her or him, I listen attentively and then move to a new subject area. I also tell them over and over that they can feel free to talk about anything with me, even if they are dissatisfied with me in some way."

Tom has initiated ways of getting the conversation going that rely on games and fun things, and then he will ease into areas that may be difficult. "Trying to keep a good solid communication with your children is very difficult if you are the noncustodial parent," says Tom. "I've called my children in the middle of the week just to say hi and tell them I love them. I call when they have a dentist appointment to see how it went, etc. And I always try for a recap of 'how was your week?' when I get them for the weekend."

No matter how close or far away you may now be living from your children, it is up to you, the parent, "to make the effort to keep the relationship going," says Dr. Robert Kurtz. "The payoff comes down the line when you're still close to your kids in adulthood."

Emotional issues are the usual things that keep people apart. People will cite money problems instead, because money is a symbol of loss. They focus on the tangible loss because they don't want to focus on the emotional loss. Try to separate the two so you can know what you are really acting on.

## Suggestions

*Don't* leave telephoning and letter writing up to your children. A young child can't write, buy stamps, or mail a letter, nor is telephoning always possible.

*Do* call, just to say hi, to ask about their day, school, teacher, friends. A good relationship with your kids is your job, built a day at a time, regardless of your marital situation.

*Do* listen when your children complain about your spouse, but let them know that their relationship with that parent is their job, not yours.

*Don't* use your children as a sounding board for your complaints about their other parent.

# CHAPTER FORTY

## *Dating*

*When is dating like bungee jumping? Now.*

"Fear is the big keyword here," says Tom, a thirty-six-year-old director of public information at a Southern university. "After my marriage of seven years broke up, I was scared of making another mistake. I kept telling myself when I got married that I knew she was the right woman for me. I knew we would never get divorced. But, I was wrong. So when I had that feeling of love for a woman again, I didn't know if I could trust myself."

Tom has had to admit that once he was finally ready to start dating, it has been fun. He hadn't dated much before his first marriage. "In fact," says Tom, "my ex-wife was only the second woman I had ever had a serious sexual relationship with. So after the divorce, I began to enjoy the process of meeting and dating women. I was constantly amazed that women would a.) find me attractive, b.) actually go out on a date with me, and occasionally, c.) sleep with me.

"Of course, I was still a bit out of touch with new dating practices. I still wanted to call the woman, ask her out, actually show up to pick her up when I said I would, and take her home and say goodnight and leave." Tom had a hard time adjusting to the "new" dating, which consisted mainly of meeting his date "out" some place and then just kind of hanging around each other with other friends.

Tom's biggest fear about dating again, in the nineties versus the late seventies, was the fear of sexually transmitted disease. "I was so inexperienced as a youngster that I don't recall ever giving this a thought, and in fact, it was never much of an issue, because I almost never took a dating situation to that level. After my divorce, when I started dating again, AIDS was always a topic of discussion during the first date or two. It was almost like we were informally checking each other out before deciding if we could move to a more physical level. It was very awkward!"

Dating is a *major* issue. When should you start to date? That depends on what is happening in your life and your children's, but most people eventually should and do begin to develop new relationships. Some welcome the idea while, for others, the thought fills them with horror.

"My marriage and divorce were painful, but I dread the idea that I might be alone for the rest of my life," says Marcia. "No matter how much I love my kids, I need adult companionship. But it's harder if you have been in an abusive relationship. My ex made me feel that nobody else would ever want me—it was his way of controlling and keeping me. Although I finally had the courage to leave him after twelve years, and am relieved to have him out of my life because I now have peace of mind, I feel isolated and alone. And yet, as much as I would like to have someone to share my life, I'm afraid of men. Someday, I hope to resolve that conflict and to start dating again."

When a parent begins to date, or become involved in an exclusive relationship, children often feel pleased *and* threatened at the same time. Or, some children are mostly relieved to see a parent happy in a new relationship, while others mostly resent it. From your child's perspective, he has already lost, to some degree, the parent who moved out. Usually that's the father. As mom, you're the most important figure in their new concept of family, i.e. security and a place to belong. They need you to be present, emotionally and physically. Children can become understandably terrified when your only focus seems to be finding your next spouse.

How your child sees a new relationship in your life has a lot to do with his age. A young child might be afraid of losing you to an outsider or may pin too much hope on every date, looking for a replacement parent, leaving themselves open to disappointment if the relationship doesn't work out.

"Just the other day," says Ralph, "I was at my ex-wife's house with our four-year-old twins. We'd agreed that she would be home by 6 o'clock after running some errands. I had dinner plans at 7 p.m.

"Suddenly it was five minutes before seven, and she still wasn't back. So I'm getting mad. Finally, able to reach her by phone, we had words—some screaming and yelling—I'm calling her selfish, etc. But there was nothing else I could do, so I put the kids in the car and drove home to collect my date, who I wasn't able to reach by phone. The two of us would drop the kids back at their mom's.

"Not wanting to upset the kids, I explained we were going to my house to meet my 'friend' and then, the two of us would take them home. One the way, my daughter asked, 'What's her name?' *Her*? 'I just thought that you were having dinner with a girl.' Obviously, it was no big deal."

Ralph's concern over his twins and dating turned out to be unjustified. However, a major source of kids' psychological distress during this time is parental conflict. For their sake, learn to negotiate, don't fight with your ex-spouse, and please, no name calling.

Regardless of your child's reaction, keep the lines of communication open. Your children's fears, fantasies, and wishes can only be handled if you know about them.

Your sexual involvement can be a sensitive issue. Many single parents, while maintaining quietly active sex lives, prefer that the children not be aware of it. However, some custodial parents who cannot hide these ongoing involvements from the children, see them as less of a threat to the parent-child relationship than remarriage would be. In any case, children are usually better equipped to handle the emotions that come up over their parents' sexuality if they think the new relationship is based on some kind of permanence and genuine affection.

Children from the same family might share the same experience yet react differently. Two brothers, both young men in their early twenties, recall:

"At twenty-two years old," says Paul, "almost any event that occurred at age eight, regardless of the level of trauma involved, is hard to completely recall. In fact, I remember very little of the day when my mother and father assembled my brother and I for an extremely rare family meeting. It was at this point that we were told that daddy will be living somewhere else, but 'you will still see each other on Fridays and weekends.'

"From what I can remember, that was all right with me. The only time I really did anything alone with my father before the divorce was on Friday evenings anyway. Therefore, little would change, except that dinner would become bearable again. Before the divorce, my only real hint of trouble was at dinnertime. That's when my parent's dirty laundry was aired. I don't know how candid they were, but it was plenty candid for me. The fighting had become incessant.

"Therefore, on that fateful evening in the kitchen, while their news didn't make me happy, there was also little sadness. I'd still get to see my dad on Friday evenings, and the house would become a little more friendly.

"After a time, my brother and I began spending weekends at my father's. I'm not sure whose idea it was, but it surely wasn't mine. It was something of a chore. For regardless of how much I enjoyed spending time with him—and believe me, I did enjoy seeing him— I hated not being able to sleep in my own bed.

"Probably the largest downside to my parents' divorce was my mother's desire to date. The idea itself did not bother me, in fact, I kind of welcomed it. The part that really bothered me was the guy she ended up dating from the time I was about ten until fourteen years old. I absolutely loathed him and to this day, still do.

"The reason I hated him so much was the fact that from the first moment on, he tried to build up an adversarial relationship with me, I guess in hopes of spurning a semiparental role for himself. It didn't work. I resented him terribly for even trying. Why couldn't he have just tried to be a friend? Occasionally we would do things together. The few times that he wasn't trying to absolutely dominate me, I actually enjoyed it.

"Regarding the entire event, the next question becomes: 'Well, how did you turn out in the end?'

"In all honesty, I turned out just fine. I am a well-adjusted, twenty-two-year-old college graduate, with hopes for the future that have not been tempered by my parents' inability to stay together. Obviously, not every day has been an easy one, but many have been. The few difficult days were an indirect, rather than a direct, result of the divorce. Both in retrospect, and at that time, I truly believe that divorce was the best thing they could have done under the circumstances."

Independent of his brother, nineteen-year-old Steve recalls: "My parents separated when I was about five. Although that time is pretty vague to me now, I do remember some feelings that I'd had. Until the day my parents told us, my brother and I, they were getting a divorce, I had no notion of what that meant or what effect it might have on my life—so the news didn't bother me. My initial reaction went no deeper than surprise.

"The divorce came at a time when the tension in the house was high. I wasn't opposed to the separation because I soon felt a sense of relief. I knew that any anger or fear that existed in the house would leave with my father.

"Initially I had a problem being with my father without the protection of my mother. I wasn't scared he would physically hurt us, but I felt he didn't understand our lives and needs like my mother did. I think the divorce changed his approach to my brother and me. Because we lived with my mother, he no longer was an equally dominant figure in our lives, and adjustments needed to be made to keep our love and respect. I now appreciate all the attempts my father made to remain a part of my life, and I love him more now than I ever did.

"My relationship with my mother is more complex, obviously due to the fact that she was my main adult figure. Before my parents divorced, I saw my mother as the protector. Not only from my dad, but from all the harsh realizations I experienced. I felt comfortable sharing my feelings any time I was bothered. After the divorce I slowly lost that bond that we shared.

"This was due in part to my growing up, becoming filled with my own insecurities which had no release. But also because of my mother's own growth. She, like I, was still searching for her strengths, and so she lacked confidence. This led her into a relationship with a completely dominant man. He took advantage of her fragile interior and turned her from the path she needed to follow. At this time, I lost much respect for my mother and felt as if I could no longer share myself with her. I also lost much trust, which is so essential in a parent-child relationship.

"Even though my real mother still existed underneath, my teenage years soon came around, and I gave up looking for her and started to discover myself. This period was very tough for us because she felt guilty about those years we missed. So she probed at my feelings too strong at a time when a teenage boy needs his mother to pull back, to give up some of the protection she wants so much to give.

"This initial resentment has since turned to acceptance and understanding. My own growth has paralleled hers, and I now hold the highest respect for my mother and love her for sticking it out with me.

"When I look back now, I don't think the divorce was a bad idea. My parents were so mismatched that problems would have arose either way. And they did what they thought was best to keep everyone happy."

It appears, for these brothers, that the divorce was handled well, and long-lasting problems were avoided. However, their mother's first romantic relationship was a disaster. Could this have been avoided? Were poor choices made in this mother's rush to establish a new relationship and sense of belonging?

"I think that men and women who date too quickly are usually too needy," said Dr. Arlene Drake, a Los Angeles psychologist, "and that when you try to replace somebody too soon, you're not really ready for love—you may be ready for sex—but not for love. I also don't think you're really seeing this person very clearly, which is how you probably got into trouble in the first place, i.e. who they are and what they have to offer. I think you're just hoping that this will be your next spouse, and your desperateness comes across.

"If you are a mother, you have to be especially careful. Not that you shouldn't date and have sex and enjoy yourself. Just don't introduce these people into your children's lives right away. Sometimes we date to test our attractiveness, and there's nothing wrong with that as long as it's kept away from the children."

It generally takes a good year or two to stabilize the emotional ups and downs of divorce and rebuild yourself. Just when you think you're feeling pretty good and that things are going along smoothly, you crash and things go down for a while. "You must stay with yourself, learn about who you are, find your inner voice, learn what you really want before you can relate to someone in an intimate way," says Drake. "It may seem great to be an instant social whirlwind, but if you don't know what you really want and need, you're going to buy the wrong package.

"When a marriage breaks up, even if it was totally the other person's fault because he or she was so horrible—they cheated, they drank, maybe were even abusive in other ways—even then, you still have to look at your part in the relationship. Really start evaluating yourself because if you don't, you'll never go on to a good relationship, you'll just re-create the last one. Why did you need to be there? What kept it going? What is it in your background that perpetrated it? Along with the normal feeling that most people have about not wanting to get divorced, what forces kept you in that marriage?

"I think that women still feel the responsibility for keeping their marriage together. Even if your ex-spouse was horrible, inside you still feel like you failed, somehow it was your job to make the marriage work."

In truth, your job is to make yourself work. When you make yourself work, then you can participate in a relationship in a healthy way which will help to make it work. "Unfortunately," says Drake, "women either take all the responsibility or none of the responsibility for the relationship. It's either black or white, good or bad. Try to take it apart, and really look at your part."

Culturally women grow up believing that marriage is their future. Slowly this perception is changing. "Men are taught about who they're going to be—a lawyer, doctor, fireman—and, of course, they'll probably get married, but that's in addition, like an accessory for a great outfit. But for women, marriage is the outfit. Because it's a woman's identity, it's such an important investment—it's a woman's life. When a woman loses a marriage, she considers herself a failure, because somehow she wasn't a good wife. All the negatives come in no matter how bad the husband was."

You are ready to start dating when you're calm and at peace with yourself, which includes the ability to spend time with yourself. This time is for you—use it to your advantage."

### Suggestions

*Don't* date too soon, while you are still feeling needy.

*Don't* make dating the only focus in your life if you have children—and, if you don't.

*Do* be sensitive to your child's feelings when you begin to date and the way in which these people are presented to them.

*Do* keep the lines of communication open with your children. Listen to their fears and help them to adapt in a positive way.

*Do* remember you are your child's role model. Act accordingly.

# CHAPTER FORTY-ONE

## *New Family Structure*
*Who's the boss?*
*-and-*

## *Social Obligations Involving Children—*
*Yes, the kids still need parents.*

Children need boundaries. They need to know who the boss is, what this person expects of them, and how they're to behave.

"As far as I'm concerned," says Tom, father of two who has his children on weekends and in between whenever possible, "I was always the boss. But, now in our new family structure, the children have many bosses. There's me and their mom, and there's the new stepdad, my ex-wife's husband, and now there's my new wife. Plus some extra grandparents here and there. The kids have to be pretty good at listening to all of us bosses and trying to do the right thing to keep us all happy. I think this may be a very good character builder for them.

"I try to give the kids a very solid vote on family activities, even major purchases. When I was contemplating marriage, I spent some serious quality time with them. We talked about the pros and cons and if we thought my new wife was a good partner for me. I wanted to know if they felt they could live with her. I think they enjoy her company more than mine some times."

Tom wants his children to know they are very important members of the family. Even though he naturally gets the last vote on most things, "they all have an important say in what's going to happen."

Not only is your family order going through changes, but social obligations involving the children come up and can, at times, leave you feeling confused about which parent should attend. Sometimes, both.

When is it appropriate to function jointly as a mom and dad? Just as soon as you can *honestly* feel comfortable being with your ex, their new lover or spouse, and even their extended family. School graduations, Little League games, college orientation, their wedding. In a nutshell, when it's THEIR special day. When their day is more important than the discomfort you might be feeling. However, if you're not sure you can keep yourself from coming to blows with your ex— keep up the *your-turn my-turn* system you developed for grade-school open houses.

"Last weekend," says Bill, "my girlfriend and I attended an engagement party for my son. My ex-wife and I have been divorced for six years, but I've been in a committed relationship for almost two.

"Everything went pretty smoothly, it was the first time my girlfriend and ex-wife spent any time together. At one point in the evening, we were all talking, the three of us, my daughter-in-law to be, and her parents, also divorced. The conversation was friendly— we had all come together to celebrate a joyful occasion. Until. My ex-wife initiated a *remember when* twist to the conversation. Before I even realized what was happening, the two of us were laughing and reminiscing about old times. After a few minutes of this, my girlfriend excused herself to visit with people.

"I realized that I was being rude and switched to another topic of conversation. I realized I had slammed an imaginary door in her face."

Knowing you will have new people and relationships in your life doesn't automatically help when it comes to protocol. What to do? When one chapter of your life has ended, although your history is part of you and has helped to make you who you are today, if you'll always remember the other person's feelings, you'll know.

## Suggestions

*Do* keep structure in your children's lives.
*Don't* discount your history, embrace it—and then, move on.

# CHAPTER FORTY-TWO

## *Life—Postdivorce*
### *Even better!*

While winding your way through separation and divorce, at times survival hardly seems possible, much less coming out the other side better and happier than you ever thought possible. Pam acknowledges she's been "through the wringer, but I am a stronger person because of it.

"In the last five years I have had a spinal fusion," says Pam, "my hubby of fifteen years left me for a young thing, I stupidly got pregnant by him a week *after* he moved out, drove myself to the hospital to have my beautiful baby girl, and was diagnosed with breast cancer a year later. I went through major chemotherapy, lost my hair, had a double mastectomy and radiation, also reconstructive surgery. I'm as sure as I'm alive that my cancer was caused by my anger and bitterness.

"I've done a major life-style change. My doctors thought the worst, but I survived it all. Life has never been better. I now have a wonderful boyfriend and lots of new hair. My children are doing great. I've even forgiven my ex—we're on better terms now than we've ever been.

"Now, two years after separation, I see my divorce as one of the most revealing, interesting, and exciting events in my life. I'm so glad to have the ability and opportunity, should I choose to take it, to look for something better if my current relationship doesn't work out."

"I can't believe it," says Sharon, "but I've been divorced for twelve years. What a growing experience it was for me. I actually found myself again. What joy! I live life funny now, and I'm always busy. It was the greatest thing that happened to me other than my two wonderful sons."

"My divorce, after fourteen years of marriage," says Michael, "will be final next month, and I'm finally beginning to feel a sense of relief. The turning point was when I realized that absolutely everyone, old friends and new, supported my decision to get a divorce. So now life awaits! It has been hell though, and I wouldn't wish the experience on anyone."

"After sixteen years of a verbally abusive marriage," says Anne, "my ex walked out and into the arms of wife number two. There's been a lot of pain, but four years of counseling later, time has healed. I sincerely believe that if the marriage isn't right, it's not right—no matter what you do. It's better to put your energy into making a new life than constantly trying to plug the holes in the old one. My dreams of running my own business and taking charge of my life are finally coming true."

"I was married in the early seventies," says Kathy "and he left me twelve years later for someone else. I'm thankful now because it gave me the courage to go through with the divorce after years of his drinking, drugging, and abusive behavior. I'm happily remarried to a wonderful man and don't regret my divorce for one minute. In fact, every year on the anniversary of the divorce, I feel like having a celebration!"

"My wife and I split up two years ago, and I'm delighted," says Norm. "It took me a while to feel comfortable with other women, but one of the things that sustained me is the knowledge that I don't have to have a wife to be happy. I have my kids and my friends and interests in my life that are my own. For me, it was fun to once again feel in ownership of my life. Unlike when I was in college and graduate school, when I thought there was a clock ticking toward a marriage deadline or I'd be lonely the rest of my life. Sure, I'd love to have another exclusive relationship someday, but I no longer feel any pressure."

Life after divorce can be great. Just think! The spouse who criticized you constantly or who obviously preferred that you weren't around (or made you feel that way), no longer is part of your daily life. You're meeting new people. People who understand just how special and enjoyable you are. This is the beginning of a new life in which respect, and perhaps even love, has been waiting for the stronger and wiser you to find them.

No one really recovers quickly and easily from a divorce. That's because recovery is a learning process, and learning takes time— time to get over your anger and sorrow, to be lonely, to make a new living environment a home, and to make friends. Don't allow yourself to stay up to your neck in remorse, regrets, and recrimination. You can leave the past behind. The choice is yours.

Gloria "Rebecca" Lintermans

"Keep Breathing."

*Sophie Tucker*

# *Acknowledgment*

I would like to offer a special thank you to the many mental health care professionals who so generously gave of their precious time and knowledge, including:

Patricia N. Allee, M.A., Los Angeles-based family therapist

Jennifer Andrews, Ph.D., M.F.C.C., a Los Angeles-based teacher and private practitioner.

Stanley Charnofsky, Ph.D., author of *When Women Leave Men: How Men Feel, How Men Heal,* (New World Library) and professor of Counseling and Educational Psychology at the University of California at Northridge, and a private practitioner.

Arlene Drake, Ph.D., M.F.C.C., Los Angeles-based psychologist in private practice.

Rusty Horn, M.S., a Manhattan-based psychotherapist and psycho-analyst specializing in parent-child issues.

Catherine Inglove, M.F.C.C., Los Angeles-based psychologist in private practice.

Arthur Kovacs, Ph.D., a Santa Monica-based psychologist in private practice.

Dr. Robert Kurtz, a staff psychologist in Cleveland State University's Counseling Center.

Dee Shepherd-Look, Ph.D., professor of psychology at California State University at Northridge.

Cyndy Lum, a psychiatric social worker for the Los Angeles Unified School District.

# Resources

## RESOURCES FOR CHILD SUPPORT ENFORCEMENT:

### CENTER FOR LAW AND SOCIAL POLICY
1616 P Street NW, Suite 450
Washington, DC 20036
Paula Roberts
Telephone (202) 328-5140
Fax (202) 328-5195

### CHILDREN'S DEFENSE FUND
25 E Street NW
Washington, DC 20001
Nancy Ebb
Telephone (202) 628-8787

### NATIONAL CENTER ON WOMEN AND FAMILY LAW
799 Broadway, Room 402
New York, NY 10003
Nancy S. Erickson
Telephone (212) 674-8200

### NATIONAL COUNCIL FOR CHILDREN'S RIGHTS
220 I Street NE, Suite 230
Washington, DC 20002
President David Levy
Telephone (202) 547-6227

### NATIONAL LEGAL RESOURCE CENTER FOR CHILD ADVOCACY & PROTECTION
American Bar Association
1800 M Street, NW
Washington, DC 20036
Telephone (202) 399-4325

**NATIONAL ORGANIZATION FOR MEN**
11 Park Place
New York, NY 10016
Telephone (212) 686-MALE

**NATIONAL ORGANIZATION FOR WOMEN**
Legal Defense and Education Fund (NOW LDEF)
99 Hudson Street
New York, NY 10013
Jenny Ann Jara
Telephone (212) 925-6635
Fax (212) 226-1066

**NATIONAL WOMEN'S LAW CENTER**
1616 P Street, NW, Suite 100
Washington, DC 20036
Duffy Cambell
Telephone (202)328-5160

**WOMEN'S LEGAL DEFENSE FUND**
1875 Connecticut Ave. NW, Suite 710
Washington, DC 20009
Judith Lichtman
Telephone (202) 986-2600

**NATIONAL CHILD SUPPORT ADVOCACY COALITION**
Box 4629
Alexandria, VA 22303 or,
Box 420
Hendersonville, TN 37077-0420
Telephone 1-800-846-2722
1-800-84N CSAC

**STEPFAMILY ASSOCIATION OF AMERICA, INC.**
28 Allegheny Avenue, Suite 1307
Baltimore, MD 21204
Telephone (301) 823-7570

**PARENTS WITHOUT PARTNERS, INC.**
401 North Michigan Avenue
Chicago, IL 60611-4267
Telephone (312) 644-6610, or
8807 Colesville Road
Silver Spring, MD 20910
Telephone 1-800-637-7974 or (301) 588-9354

Support groups for single parents.

### SINGLE MOTHERS BY CHOICE
P.O. Box 1642, Gracie Square Station
New York, NY 10028
Telephone (212) 988-0993

### SINGLE PARENTS RESOURCE CENTER
1165 Broadway
New York, NY 10001
Telephone (212) 213-0047

### SINGLE PARENTS SOCIETY (NY and NJ)
527 Cinnaminson Avenue
Palmyra, NJ 08065
Telephone (609) 424-8872

### THE SISTERHOOD OF BLACK SINGLE MOTHERS, INC.
1360 Fulton St., Room 413
Brooklyn, NY 11216
Telephone 1-800-338-3732

### WOMEN ON THEIR OWN, INC. (W.O.T.O.)
P.O. Box 1026
Willingboro, NJ 08046
Telephone (609) 871-1499

Support, networking, advocacy, quarterly newsletter. Loan program.

## ADDITIONAL RESOURCES:

### CHILD SUPPORT ENFORCEMENT SERVICES, INC.
110 East 59th Street
New York, NY 10022
Telephone 1-800-KIDS740 (543-7740)

This is a private organization which helps locate absent fathers and collects past-due child support. Child-support court order and custody of child necessary.

### SUPERVISED FAMILY SERVICES
3442 Faxon Avenue
Memphis, TN 38122
Telephone (901) 324-6093

This organization provides extended visitation of five to seven hours to noncustodial parent in instances where they have been denied access to their children due to abuse allegations. Only court-ordered cases accepted.

**FIND DAD**
Box 2645
Fairfax, VA 22031-0645
Telephone (703) 803-9700
Fax (703) 803-8212
Helpline 1-800-925-0905 (1-800-PAY-MOMS)

A private organization, FIND DAD helps locate the absent parent and collects child-support arrearages. Child-support court order necessary. Not eligible if currently receiving AFDC payments.

**THE ACCOUNTS RETRIEVABLE SYSTEM, INC.**
2050 Bellmore Avenue
Bellmore, NY 11710-5600
Telephone 1-800-FAR-IOUS (1-800-327-4687) or
(516) 783-6566

This is a full-service collection agency that locates noncustodial parents and collects past-due child support, alimony, and maintenance. Searches for assets including bank accounts, motor vehicles, retirement plans, real estate, and employment. No application fee, no costs advanced by clients, if they do not collect, no charge—otherwise 33 percent of amount collected.

**NATIONAL INSTITUTE FOR RESPONSIBLE FATHERHOOD & FAMILY DEVELOPMENT**
8555 Hough Avenue
Cleveland, OH 44106
Telephone (216) 791-1468

The first organization of its kind to recognize the needs of young fathers. They seek to create and maintain an environment in which fathers can develop the skills they need to provide quality lives for their children and the mothers of their children.

**HUSBANDS AGAINST DIRTY DIVORCE**
P.O. Box 85885
Seattle, WA 98145
Telephone (206) 743-3300

This organization provides information on visitation rights, divorce laws, custody, and paternity.

### GENETIC DESIGN, INC.
7017 Albert Park Road
Greensboro, NC 27409-9654
Pam Hairston, private sales
Telephone 1-800-247-9540 Ex. 3939

Established in 1986, this is the largest genetic-testing lab in the world (paternity, forensic, medical diagnostics, and therapeutics) combining accurate testing with prompt, quality services according to The Children's Foundation in Washington, D.C. Write or call to receive their private paternity referral guide.

## WRITTEN MATERIALS FOR CHILD SUPPORT:

If you contact the organizations listed above, you should request a publications listing. Listed below are a sampling of publications available from these and other organizations:

### CENTER FOR LAW AND SOCIAL POLICY
1616 P Street, Suite 450
Washington, DC 20036
Telephone (202) 328-5140

*Child Support and Beyond: Mapping a Future for America's Low Income Children,* 20 pages. Price $5.

*Women, Poverty and Child Support,* 156 pages. Price $15.

*Turning Promises Into Realities,* 107 pages. Price $15.

*Childhood's End: What Happens to Children When Child Support Obligations Are Not Enforced,* 34 pages. Price $10.

### DEPARTMENT OF HEALTH AND HUMAN SERVICES
Administration for Children and Families
370 L'Enfant Promenade SW
Washington, DC 20047
Telephone (202) 401-9370

### OFFICE OF CHILD SUPPORT ENFORCEMENT
Reference Center
Telephone (202) 401-9383

## MATERIALS—FREE AND OTHERWISE—ON THE CHILD-SUPPORT OBLIGATION INCLUDE:

*Bankruptcy and Support Enforcement—How to Make Sure It Stays Owed to the Kids*

*The Changing Face of Child Support Enforcement: Incentives to Work with Young Parents*

*Child Support: An Annotated Legal Bibliography*

*Child Support and Alimony*

*Child Support Enforcement in the Military*

*Child Support Report* (compiled monthly)

*Compilation of State Best Practices in Child Support*

*Developing Effective Procedures for Pro Se Modification of Child Support Awards*

*Designing a Model Child Support Enforcement Program—A Resource Allocation Workbook*

*Effective Use of Liens in Child Support Cases*

*Essentials for Attorneys in Child Support Enforcement: Second Edition*

*Federal Parent Locator Service*

*Federal Tax Refund Offset Program*

*Fifteenth Annual Report to Congress*

*A Guide About Child Support Enforcement for Credit Grantors*

*Guide to Service Quality Analysis in Child Support Enforcement*

*The Income Withholder's Role in Child Support*

*Interstate Child Support Remedies*

*Kids, They're Worth Every Penny: Handbook on Child Support Enforcement*

*A New Vision: Self-Sufficiency in the Nineties*

*Paternity Establishment: Third Edition*

*Research Compendium*

*Service of Process*

*State Budget Implications: Child Support Enforcement*

*The Treatment of Multiple Family Cases Under State Child Support Guidelines*

*Tribal and State Court Reciprocity in the Establishment and Enforcement of Child Support*

*Wage Withholding for Child Support: An Employer's Guide*

*Child Support: A Complete, Up-to-Date Authoritative Guide to Collecting Child Support,* Marianne Takas (New York: Harper & Row, 1985). This book is available in bookstores or write to Marianne Takas, 19 Goldstar Road, Cambridge MA 02140. $6.95 paperback.

*Juvenile and Family Court JOURNAL, Special Issue: Child Support Enforcement,* Fall 1985/Vol. 36 No. 3. Back copies of the journal are available from: Fred B. Rothman & Company Law Books, 10368 W. Centennial Road, Littleton, CO 80123.

*The Myth of Child Support and Alimony, 1986.* Approximately six pages. Requests for this publication, along with a check for $3 to Women's Legal Defense Fund, 1875 Connecticut Avenue NY, Suite 710, Washington, DC 20009.

*The Child Support Survivor's Guide,* by Barry T. Schnell. Requests for this publication, along with a check for $7.95, should be sent to: Consumer Awareness Learning Laboratory, P.O. Box 952, Salem, NJ 08079.

*Improving Child Support Practice.* Washington, DC. The American Bar Association, 1986 (549-0054). Price $45 plus $2 handling charge per order. This is a two-volume set totaling 1150 pages.

*America's Children at Risk: A National Agenda for Legal Action.* A report of the American Bar Association Presidential Working Group on the Unmet Legal Needs of Children and Their Families. (1993) The price is $8 plus $2.48 shipping and handling.

Requests for these publications should be sent to:

**THE AMERICAN BAR ASSOCIATION**
Order Fulfillment, 549
750 North Lake Shore Drive
Chicago, IL 60611

**NATIONAL LEGAL RESOURCE CENTER FOR CHILD ADVOCACY & PROTECTION**
American Bar Association
1800 M Street, NW
Washington, DC 20036
Telephone (202) 399-4325

A publications catalog is available from the National Legal Resource Center for Child Advocacy and Protection. Topics include child abuse and exploitation, permanency planning, foster care, adoption, interstate child custody, and parental kidnapping. The ABA Child Support Project cannot answer individual requests for advice. Assistance is limited to providing publications and other reference materials.

NOW LDEF (see above address and telephone number) has several publications on the child-support obligation which are available for $5 to defray costs, including:

"Fact Sheet on Child Support Enforcement"

"Information Sheet on Enforcing Child Support Orders"

"Selected Bibliography on Child Support"

*Child Support Guidelines: An Introductory Handbook for Advocates.* Each state must adopt numerical formulas or guidelines for setting child-support award amounts. This handbook explains the guidelines issue and its importance for custodial parents and children.

*Child Support in America—Practical Advice for Negotiating—and Collecting—a Fair Settlement,* Joseph I. Lieberman (New Haven: Yale University Press, 1986). $14.95 hardback.

*Child Support Assurance: Making Child Support Work for Children,* by Julia Quiroz and Nancy Ebb, published by the Children's Defense Fund. To order, write to: T'Wana Lucas, Children's Defense Fund, 25 E Street, NW, Washington, DC 20001.

## PUBLICATIONS ON RELATED SUBJECTS

*Child Custody—A Complete Guide for Concerned Mothers,* Marianne Takas (New York: Harper and Row, 1987). $7.95 paperback or $15.95 hardback.

**NATIONAL CENTER FOR MISSING AND EXPLOITED CHILDREN**
2101 Wilson Boulevard, Suite 500
Arlington, VA 22201
Telephone (703) 235-3900

Toll-free Information HOTLINE: 1-800-843-5678, for individuals who have information which could lead to the location of a missing child.

The National Center for Missing and Exploited Children has a national clearinghouse that provides information on the issue of missing and exploited children. Reading includes:

*Parental Kidnapping—How to Prevent an Abduction and What to Do if Your Child is Abducted.*

*Directory of Support Services and Resources for Missing and Exploited Children*

*Selected State Legislation* (state laws to protect children)

*Child Protection* (safety tips)

*Information Brochure*

The following publications are available from the Women's Legal Defense Fund (see above address). They are out of print but available at the cost of photocopying.

*Custody and Visitation: Their Relationship to Establishing and Enforcing Support,* 1985, 4 pages.

*Why Mothers Are Losing: A Brief Analysis of Criteria Used in Child Custody Determinations,* 1983, 9 pages.

The following publications are available:

*The Report Card,* a study on the child-support systems in each state, written primarily for state legislators.

*Barriers,* a study on why women don't seek support from absent fathers.

Following is a list of some of the many publications and voice cassettes available from the National Council for Children's Rights, also known as Children Rights Council, a nonprofit organization strengthening families and assisting children of separation and divorce. Write to them for a complete publications list at: 200 I Street, Suite 230, Washington, DC 20002.

*Crisis in Family Law: Children as Victims of Divorce,* 32 pages. (R101). Price is $6.40.

*Joint Custody,* 28 pages. (R102). Price is $5.60.

*Synopses of Sole and Joint Custody Series,* 27 pages. (R103). Price is $5.40.

*Anti-Kidnapping and Anti-Removal Report,* 75 pages. (R107). Price is $15.

*Fifty-Six Points in Favor of Joint Custody,* 6 pages. (R108). Price is $1.20.

*Needs of Children of Divorce.* (V101) Custody, visitation, Aid to Families with Dependent Children, women's issues, and other matters are discussed on 3 voice cassettes.

*Implementing Joint Custody Agreements.* (V102). Price is $7.80.

*Challenging the Washington, D.C. Child Support Guidelines,* 50 pages. (L104). Price is $10.

*Review of Child Support Guidelines,* 65 pages. (R115). Price $13.

*Helping Your Child Succeed After Divorce,* by Florence Bienenfeld, Ph.D. A resource book depicting the impact of divorce on children. 206 pages. Price $9.95.

*Mom's House, Dad's House,* by Isolina Ricci, Ph.D. Making shared custody work: how parents can make two homes for their children after divorce. 270 pages. Price $8.95.

*Sharing The Children,* by Robert Adler, Ph.D. Shows how mom, dad, and children can all come out winners. 254 pages. Price $7.95.

*Divorce Book For Parents,* by Vicky Lansky. Advice on how to help your children survive and even thrive. 225 pages. Price $4.50.

*Families Are Forever,* by Nathan Schaefer, M.D. How to establish new and successful patterns of parenting, regardless of your marital situation. 160 pages. Price $9.95.

*Growing Up Again, Parenting Ourselves, Parenting Our Children,* by Jean Illsley Clarke and Connie Dawson. For those who grew up with bad parenting habits they do not want to pass on to their children. 186 pages. Price $12.95.

*The Dynamics of Divorce,* by Florence Kaslow, Ph.D., and Lita Linzer Schwartz, Ph.D. Addresses the different impact that divorce has on all involved; details tasks to be mastered at each state of the divorce cycle and the kinds of therapy that are of the most help. 329 pages. Price $35.

*Helping Children Cope With Divorce,* By Edward Teyber, Ph.D. Describes the stress children experience and explains how best to shield them from the parents' own conflict. 200 pages. Price $20.

*For The Sake of The Children,* by Kris Kline and Stephen Pew, Ph.D., Insights and advice on how parents can cooperate after divorce. 220 pages. Price $17.95.

*Families, Crisis And Caring,* by T. Berry Brazelton, M.D. Talks about the involved father, parental rivalry, grandparenting, the loss of a parent, fathering alone, stepfamilies, illness in the family, helping the other children cope, adoption, and when to seek help. 252 pages. Price $18.

*The Best Parent Is Both Parents,* edited by David L. Levy. Information on parenting support, access, and school-based programs to help children. 160 pages. Price $9.95.

*Families A\*P\*A\*R\*T\*,* by Melinda Blau. Ten keys to successful co-parenting. 349 pages. $22.95.

Books Especially For Kids:

*Dinosaurs Divorce,* by Laurene Krasny Brown and Marc Brown. Cartoon style, story form to help children ages 4-12 understand divorce words and what they mean, why parents divorce, how children feel, and having two homes. 31 pages. Price $3.95.

*My Mom And Dad Are Getting A Divorce,* by Florence Bienenfeld, Ph.D. Cartoon style, story form focuses on children ages 4-12. Helps them through the feelings of sadness, loss, hurt, anger, guilt, helplessness, and fear triggered by a divorce. 38 pages. Price $3.95.

*I Think Divorce Stinks,* by Marcia Lebowitz. Cartoon style, story form that helps children recognize that it is appropriate to have negative feelings about divorce and to express these feelings. 16 pages. Price $4.95.

*Divorce Happens To The Nicest Kids,* by Michael Prokop, M.Ed., school psychologist. An illustrated book explaining divorce in a positive and reassuring manner. For kids ages 3-15 and adults. 220 pages. Price $11.95.

*Changing Families,* by David Fassler, M.D., Michele Lash, M.Ed., A.T.R., and Sally Ives, Ph.D. A large, workbook-type guide that takes kids and grownups through all phases of the family separation, divorce, new family, and feelings. 180 pages. Price $14.95.

*My Mother's House, My Father's House,* by C.B. Christiansen, illustrated by Irene Trivas. The story of a little girl who is comfortable in both her mother's house and her father's house, and her ideas about how she will love when she grows up. 34 pages. Price $3.95.

*Questions From Dad,* by Dwight Twilley, singer and songwriter. Completing the highly praised questionnaire will help children communicate with their parents long distance. 190 pages. Price $16.95.

*How To Survive Your Parents' Divorce: Kids Advice To Kids,* by Dayle Kimball, Ph.D. More than 250 young people and 20 counselors share insights. 160 pages. Price $9.95.

## SCHOOL PROGRAMS

BANANA SPLITS: a school/parent support program for children of divorce. Entering voluntarily and with parental permission, "Splits" kids are grouped by age and grade level and meet every two or three weeks to air the frustrations and successes of their altered family lives. A volunteer teacher or counselor guides discussions and offers individual attention when a serious problem or crisis is perceived. But a big part of the program is when other kids help a group member move through a particularly tough situation such as a child-custody hearing or learning to get along with a stepparent.

This program offers more than group counseling, however. Its "curriculum" includes special art projects which help younger children express their concerns through drawing; in other activities, they air their anxieties by playing with stuffed animals and toys. Older children and youths do several activities: develop a more sophisticated graffiti wall as a springboard for discussion of common problems; act as peer counselors as well as set up activities for younger "latch-key" children; construct collages; write and act out skits; do paintings; and plan social activities for the whole group (e.g. an end-of-year "Banana Splits Picnic"). Finally, the program contains directions for setting up parent groups which meet in the evenings.

Banana Splits is organized and presented in a three-ring notebook with eight tab sections and 116 pages. At no cost to participants, the notebook cost is $40.

For more information contact:

**INTERACT**
Box 997-BS93
Lakeside, California 92040
(619) 448-1474 or toll-free 1-800-359-0961

## HOME PROGRAMS

### INTELECOM
Plaza Center
150 E. Colorado Boulevard, Suite 300
Pasadena, California 91105-1937
Telephone (818) 796-7300
Fax (818) 577-4282

Videotape series *Portrait of a Family.* Each half-hour videotape is $29.95; shipping and tape cost included. These videotapes are for private home viewing only with text materials sold separately.

*Portrait of a Family,* produced by the southern California Consortium, takes a close look at marriage and family with a focus on traditional families, single-parent families, stepfamilies, family without children, dual-worker marriages, and cohabiting couples.

Module IV: The Family in Transition offers three videotapes of interest: Number 21 - **The Strained Knot/Families in Crisis**; Number 22 - **Irreconcilable Differences/Separation and Divorce**; and Number 23 - **Single, Head of Household/The Single Parent Family.**

## DIVORCE SUPPORT GROUPS:

NORTH AMERICAN ASSOCIATION OF SEPARATED AND DIVORCED CATHOLICS (founded 1975): 1100 S. Goodman St., Rochester, NY 14620. Telephone (716) 271-1320.

DIVORCE ANONYMOUS (founded 1987): 2600 Colorado Ave., Ste. 270, Santa Monica, CA 90404. Telephone (310) 315-6538.

THE FRIENDS (founded 1971): P.O. Box 389, Fargo, ND 58107. Telephone (701) 235-7341. A "bank" of people who have been through various life crises, who are matched with someone undergoing a similar problem.

THE SINGLE LIFE (founded 1972): 85 Central St., Waltham, MA 02154. Telephone (617) 891-3750. A support organization of divorced, separated, widowed, and never-married men and women.

Please note that this list does not include every organization, private program, or literature that deals with the various aspects of divorce. Inclusion on this list does not constitute endorsement by the author or publishers of this book.

## SOURCES

*Caring About Kids: When Parents Divorce,* U.S. DEPARTMENT OF HEALTH AND HUMAN SERVICES, National Institute of Mental Health—Public Health Service, *Alcohol, Drug Abuse, and Mental Health Administration,* 1981.

*Children of Divorce,* Policy Implications From NICHD Research; CENTER FOR POPULATION RESEARCH, National Institute of Child Health and Human Development, NATIONAL INSTITUTES OF HEALTH (NIH), May 1993.

*A Child's View on Divorce, The Daily News,* April 3, 1994, CHICAGO TRIBUNE News Release.

*The Children of Divorce,* by Linda Bird Francke with Diane Sherman in Washington, Pamela Ellis Simons in Chicago, Palela Abramson in San Francisco, Marsha Zabarsky in Boston, Janet Huck in Los Angeles and Lisa Whitman in New York, *Newsweek,* February 11, 1980.

*What's Happening to the Family? Interactions Between Demographic and Institutional Change,* Population Association of America, 1990 Presidential Address, Larry L. Bumpass, Center for Demography and Ecology, University of Wisconsin, Madison, Wisconsin 53706, *Demography,* Vol. 27, No. 4, November 1990.

*Handbook on Child Support Enforcement, Collecting Child Support, Federal Tax Refund Program,* and *Federal Parent Locator Service,* U.S. DEPARTMENT OF HEALTH AND HUMAN SERVICES, Administration for Children and Families, Office of Child Support Enforcement.

*The Constitutional Right To Be A Parent,* citations compiled by: Stuart A. Miller, senior legislative analyst for the American Fathers Coalition.

*Empirical Studies Relation To Access/Visitation With Regard To The Family Dynamics of Divorce, Separation and Illegitimacy,* "A special report to the 1994 Virginia Legislature," Stuart A. Miller, White House liaison, American Fathers Coalition - assistant director, Children's Rights Coalition of Virginia - director of governmental affairs, Texas Fathers Alliance - executive director, Family Resolution Council - senior legislative analyst for the American Fathers Coalition, and Mark Price, Esq., constitutional counsel - American Fathers Coalition.

*Dating Goes Beyond the Strange,* by Judy Markey, Life-style columnist, WOMEN, March 13, 1994, *Daily News.*

*Marriages and Families*: Making Choices and Facing Change, Fifth Edition, by Mary Ann Lamanna and Agnes Riedmann, ITP, Wadsworth Publishing Company, Belmont, CA.

*Family Advocate,* A Practical Journal by the ABA Family Law Section, *"Your Divorce: A Guide Through the Legal Process,"* Summer 1992, Vol 15, No. 1, AMERICAN BAR ASSOCIATION

*The Constitutional Right To Be A Parent,* Citations compiled by: Stuart A. Miller, Children's Rights Council - 1994.

*Divorce Recovery: Healing the Hurt Through Self-Help and Professional Support,* Allan J. Adler, M.D. and Christine Archambault, a Bantam Premium Book and The Psychiatric Institutes of America - The PIA Press, 1990.

*The Divorce Book For Men And Women: A Step-By-Step Guide To Gaining Your Freedom Without Losing Everything Else* by Harriet Newman Cohen and Ralph Gardner, Jr., Avon Books, 1994.

*Adult Children of Divorce Speak Out: About Growing Up With—And Moving Beyond—Parental Divorce,* by Claire Berman, Simon & Schuster, 1991.

*How to Survive the Loss of a Love* by Melba Colgrove, Ph.D., Harold H. Bloomfield, M.D., and Peter McWilliams, published by Prelude Press, 8159 Santa Monica Boulevard, Los Angeles, CA 90046, 1-800-LIFE-101.

*Compton's Encyclopedia,* Online Edition, downloaded from America Online, July 20, 1994.

*Our Turn: The Good News About Women and Divorce,* by Christopher L. Hayes, Ph.D., Deborah Anderson, Melinda Blau, Pocket Books, 1993.

*Creative Divorce: A New Opportunity For Personal Growth,* by Mel Krantz-ler, M. Evans and Company, 1974.

*How to Grand-parent,* by Dr. Fitzhaugh Dodson with Paul Reuben, Harper & Row, Publishers, 1981.

*A Book for Grand-Mothers* by Ruth Goode, Macmillan Publishing Co., Inc., 1976.

*What to Do When Your Son or Daughter Divorces: A New Guide of Hope and Help for Parents of Adult Children,* by Dorothy Weiss Gottlieb,

Inez Bellow Gottlieb, and Marjorie A. Slavin, M.S.W., Bantam Books, 1988.

*The Parents Book About Divorce* by Richard A. Gardner, M.D., Doubleday & Company, Inc., 1977.

*Sharing The Children: How To Resolve Custody Problems and Get On With Your Life* by Robert E. Adler, Ph.D., Adler & Adler, 1988.

*How To Divorce Your Wife: The Man's Side of Divorce* by Forden Athearn, Doubleday & Company, Inc., 1976.